Everything I Wanted to Know About Spirituality but Didn't Know How to Ask

The picture above, known as the Flammarion Engraving, reveals a seeker breaking through the veil of our physical world to view the inner workings of the Universe. This image was first seen in a book published in 1888 by Camille Flammarion called L'*atmosphère: Météorologie Populaire* ("The Atmosphere: Popular Meteorology"). The artist is unknown. The cover background is a colorized, inverted, and adjusted version of the original.

Also by Peter Santos

Peter's spiritual novel, *The Light Beyond the Shadows: A Tale of Awakening*, is an intimate, mystical tale of personal growth and spiritual evolution that expresses timeless wisdom as it progresses through seven distinct lessons corresponding to the body's seven energy centers.

For a basic introduction to some of the topics contained in this book, see *The Little Book of Spiritual Growth: A Straightforward Primer on Energy, God, Spirit, Soul & Ego*.

For an inspiring, spiritual story with a hands-on lesson for your child, see the children's book, *Little Gifts: The Adventures of a Pigeon-angel*.

Everything I Wanted to Know About Spirituality but Didn't Know How to Ask

A Spiritual Seeker's Guidebook

Second Edition

Peter Santos

Spirit Speaks Publishing

Everything I Wanted to Know About Spirituality but Didn't Know How to Ask: A Spiritual Seeker's Guidebook
Second Edition

Original edition copyright © 2015 by Peter Santos.
Second edition copyright © 2016 by Peter Santos.

All rights reserved. No part of this book may be reproduced or transmitted in any form or manner whatsoever without express written permission in writing from the publisher and copyright holder, except in the case of brief quotations embodied in critical articles and reviews. No part of this book may be used in any manner for purposes of training artificial intelligence (AI) technologies or for generative AI use without the author's express, written permission.

No AI was used in the creation of this book.

Published by Spirit Speaks Publishing
Berlin, Vermont
www.spiritspeakspublishing.com

For additional copies, please contact the publisher.

Library of Congress Control Number: 2016911270

ISBN-13: 978-0989610742

The universe beyond the sun and stars and all the thoughts of which you can conceive belong to you.

– A Course in Miracles,
Original Edition,
M-20.6:11

Contents

Preface xiii

Introduction xvii

1 Overview 3

2 A Primer on Energy 9

3 Body, Soul & Spirit 17
    Physical Body 18
    Mental Body 19
    Emotional Body 20
    Feeling Nature 21
    Soul 21
    Higher Self 23

4 Three Energies of Being 25

5 God & Ego 31

6 Healing 39
    Spiritual Healing 42
    Other Healing 44

7 Prayer 49

8 Meditation 51

	Guided Meditation	53
9	There Is Only Now	57
10	Reincarnation	63
11	Perceived Karma	69
12	Life Contracts & Free Will	73
13	Seeing From a Higher Context	79
14	Transforming Baggage	85
15	Asking for Help	93
16	Reframing	99
17	Grounding, Centering & Protecting	103
	Grounding	103
	Centering	104
	Protecting	105
18	Intention & Manifesting	111
19	I AM & Affirmations	117
20	Trust & Discernment	121
21	Attachment, Addiction & Detachment	127
	Attachment & Addiction	127
	Detachment	130
22	Judgment	133
23	Fear & Forgiveness	139
24	Dreams	145
25	Distractions	153

26	Care of the Physical	159
27	Disconnecting to Connect	167
28	Being Uncomfortable	171
29	Phenomena	177
30	Discernment with Teachers	181
31	Miscellaneous Thoughts	187
	Mistakes	187
	Channeling	188
	The Christ	189
	The Holy Spirit	190
	Heaven & Hell	190
	Religion	191
	Ceremony & Ritual	192
	Sex	193
	Money	194
	Vegetarianism & Other Diets	196
	Relationships & Children	198
32	Our Choice	201
33	Summary	205
34	Not an End, but a Beginning	211

Preface

Decades ago, I would have never imagined I could write a book like this. Although I was interested in spirituality, my perception was that a regular life and a spiritual life could not be integrated. I thought I had to choose one or the other, one *over* the other, and I wasn't ready to give up what I saw as my "normal" life. Over time, I began to realize that nothing was further from the truth.

For many years I was an analyst, sitting in front of a computer in an office cubicle working on spreadsheets day after day. Yeah, I was *that* guy. Meanwhile, unbeknownst to my colleagues, I was studying spirituality and healing in my spare time, as it had been an interest of mine since my late teens. As the years passed, I found myself increasingly dissatisfied with my vocation and began to see that difficult work situations were just a mirror to my internal discontent. I knew there was more for me to do, more for me to *be*, outside of the cubicle. Eventually, I felt this inner call strongly enough to move me to quit my job, change careers, and pursue a more spiritual life, one that began to put into practice what I had assimilated through my years of study. Despite some bumps along the road, the results of this change have made me more focused, happier, more engaged with life, and further aligned with my Spirit within. I am a *very* different person than I was five or ten years ago.

The material presented in this book is information I wish I had seen when I began my spiritual path. While I doubt I would have fully understood the concepts contained herein at that time, the book would have been a welcome resource while on my journey, as it would have provided useful clarifications to the many different and sometimes conflicting spiritual teachings I encountered. The compilation of this material sprang from my desire to simplify and illuminate to *myself* what I learned about spirituality over the years, with all the impractical and unnecessary teachings and distractions stripped away. Time and experience has allowed these understandings to move from my head to my heart, from knowing them intellectually to integrating them into my being, allowing me to *feel* and understand how to apply them to everyday living.

This book is a collection of the basic knowledge that I believe can produce tangible spiritual growth if it is put into practice. Many people *say* they want to lighten their energies, know the divine within, and return to God, but they have difficulty *living* those ideals. Applying them in a chaotic world that demands our attention at every turn can be a challenge. Although everyone's journey is unique, most paths lead through certain revelations and insights that I believe can be brought to awareness more quickly by practicing and living the concepts contained within these pages.

Preface

I invite you to do what I have done, to look at yourself in a mirror and ask, "What do I really believe and am I truly a living example of it?" We may have all the latest yoga clothing, have a "Jesus Saves" bumper sticker on our car, follow the latest inspirational or spiritual teacher, or collect spiritual books for our bookshelf. Yet, if we go home and judge our neighbors or fight with our spouse about ridiculous details that mean nothing in the grand scheme of things (maybe while still in our yoga clothing!), we are not living to the fullest potential of who we can be. And who are we really fooling but ourselves?

Spiritual growth can present challenges, but through them we can learn and progress on our path. Our development isn't always clean and pretty, soft and fuzzy, warm and nurturing. When old issues surface that need to be cleared out of our physical, emotional, and mental bodies, often we must put on our hip boots and wade into the swamp with the snakes and alligators to wrestle a deeper understanding from them. Not always, but often.

What follows is a bare-bones, honest assessment of the spiritual path and how to integrate it with our so-called "normal" lives. In truth, spirituality and our day-to-day living work together. They cannot be separated. Our spirituality even ***determines*** the quality of our life.

Please know that although I wrote this book for myself to clarify my own thoughts, occasionally I use "you." More than anything, it's really a "we" because we are all in it together.

My hope is that this presentation of basic spiritual concepts and practical ideas on how to live them will bring greater peace and love into your awareness. If you find the messages, perspectives, and exercises useful for elevating your energy and living a more positive life, then I'm grateful. Your brighter energy will spread and help make the world a better place. I appreciate you joining me on this journey toward living our truth. We can't do it alone, and it starts with us.

Peter Santos
January 2015

Introduction

This guidebook is designed to give the reader a basic understanding of practical and useful concepts and terms that are likely to be encountered on the spiritual path, along with some ideas and beliefs that may be more esoteric but are exceptionally helpful. Also provided are key questions and tools that are useful for working through the mental, emotional, and spiritual blocks that inhibit true spiritual growth.

The book does not digress into historic, scientific, philosophical, or theological explanations. There are countless other books that can explain the ideas herein from the context of those disciplines. This book, rather, is a straightforward guidebook of helpful information and effective tools that can help us understand what we need to do in order to lighten our energy and discover and realize who and what we are in truth.

As physical human beings we wear a coat of fallibility. We do not see ourselves as perfect but that is what we are, a pure expression of the divine, just covered up with our humanness. When we can see and experience the truth behind the curtain, beyond the veil of the physical, we can begin to anchor that truth in our current lives through *being* it.

Everything I Wanted to Know About Spirituality . . .

You may be reading this book because the title intrigues you or you're a spiritual seeker following your path. You may have read countless books on a variety of spiritual concepts while holding down a full time job, taking care of the kids, and managing your "real" life. You may even do yoga, eat a vegan diet, or go to a few meditation classes or retreats. Great! This book is designed to assist you in understanding how those and other activities, events, settings, interests, and circumstances fit into your spiritual development. It provides tools for your spiritual toolbox that will positively enhance your practice and help you live the ideals to which you aspire. For all of us, practicing the exercises and living the concepts that follow can lead to a transformation of our being, rippling out to others, to better the world we all share.

In this second edition, there are several questions and exercises at the end of each chapter. They are designed to elicit responses that take the reader to a deeper understanding of each topic covered and help integrate and apply the material into daily living to foster spiritual growth. Many of the questions are the same for each chapter, but each can be applied specifically to the topic at hand.

As much as answering all the questions and doing every exercise might be beneficial, people learn in many different ways and some questions or exercises may not resonate or apply to you. However, note that avoiding certain chapters' questions may also be an indication that your ego knows that having a better understanding of

Introduction

those topics will threaten its voice, so it may make you think that a question is a waste of time and not helpful. In addition, you may find that some questions are repetitive for the same chapter, but their wording aims to produce particular feelings and responses. Whatever the case, proceed slowly and take the time to do what you can.

In the process of working through the chapters, you may uncover thoughts, emotions, and energies that have been long forgotten, or you may encounter deeply entrenched issues triggered by the responses you provide. If at any time you feel challenged enough to feel overwhelmed, please seek assistance from a professional counselor or therapist, particularly a psycho-spiritual counselor if possible. They can be enormously helpful in giving context and guidance to your struggles and can facilitate working through blocks to your growth.

It is recommended that you purchase a separate writing journal to accompany this book so you have all the space you need to record your answers and reflections.

Thank you for embarking on this journey.

Everything I Wanted to Know About Spirituality but Didn't Know How to Ask

~ Chapter 1 ~

Overview

What we achieve inwardly will change outer reality.

– Plutarch

To provide some context to the pages that follow, below are some concepts that you will come to understand as you progress on the spiritual path. Becoming familiar with them is the first step to being able to integrate them into your life, for most things come into existence by first being conceived of in the mind. In truth, we are just calling these understandings into our awareness once again.

It is possible to *not* learn and *not* comprehend these concepts and still progress on the path, but since spiritual seekers are usually actively *seeking* information, then their path (*your* path because you are reading this) is one of acquiring spiritual knowledge and understanding, hopefully to put it into practice to better your life and the lives around you.

- No matter how we label it—God, universal intelligence, inner light, Spirit within, etc.—there exists a

universal power that is beyond what our conscious mind can comprehend.
- As a seed contains the full potential of the tree, each of us contains all the light, perfection, and potency of God, the universal power.
- We all are on a path of "returning" to our oneness with the divine source, even though we never left it.
- We feel guilt and fear for perceiving that we separated from God, but we never did. God has always been in us and around us in everything that exists, because we are in God.
- The more we remember that God never left us and genuinely live from that perspective, the more we feel and know our divine connection.
- Because God is part of each of us, we as individuals create as God does with God's full and perfect creative power. However, most of the time we *miscreate* because we are not creating out of perfect love in alignment with God.
- The three-dimensional world as we know it is an elaborate illusion, a reflection of mankind's collective conscious and subconscious miscreations and misperceptions. It is a fantasy, like a dramatic television show, because it is not "real life." However, it is the greatest place for us to learn the lessons we need to learn to realize our connection with God.
- What we perceive as our outer world is a mirror of our inner world. Our internal energies invite external

circumstances that reflect the sum total of all the energies we carry.

- Both the positive and negative in the three-dimensional world were created by mankind, except for expressions of *perfect* joy, peace, and love, which are divine and beyond illusion.
- The duality of positive and negative becomes subsumed in oneness. There are no opposites in the totality and absolute perfection of the oneness that we know as divine.
- Creating and perceiving from the divinity within us is Truth, which is beyond the physical world. Truth and illusion cannot coexist because perfect Truth destroys illusion.
- There are no coincidences and no mistakes. Every role has a purpose and every path has merit. Everything we do and experience is for learning to remember our union with God.
- When we can trust in that union and allow the Spirit within to express through us, life becomes joyful and loving as divine guidance unerringly works for our highest and best.
- Time is a three-dimensional concept utilized by mankind to perceive cause and effect. Because only the present moment ever exists, there is no time as we know it. Nevertheless, the progression of time is used as a tool for learning.
- The ego is a non-spiritual aspect of ourselves solely interested in self-preservation. It perceives the in-

creasing awakening to our inner light as a threat to its survival and as such, will subvert our growth at every turn.
- Thoughts, emotions, and memories work together under the direction of the ego to keep us from being truly present in the Now.
- Spiritual growth is about getting closer to recognizing and living from the divine within in the present moment. Always.

Because nearly all of us cannot make the leap of faith to trust the information above on a deep, knowing level, we need to take steps to prepare our minds and hearts to accept it. The following chapters attempt to accomplish this.

Questions:

1. How did you feel as you read the chapter? Did it support or challenge your previous understanding of the concepts?

2. What stood out to you?

3. Make three columns in your journal: True, Maybe True, and Not True. Capture each bullet point from the chapter in a few of your own words and list them in the three columns: ones you recognize as true, ones you see as maybe true, and ones you would say are not true. Does a theme stand out?

4. What topics do you feel you need (or desire) to understand more? Is there something in your past that you feel might be inhibiting your acceptance of particular concepts?

5. How might you apply any of this material in your life?

~ Chapter 2 ~

A Primer on Energy

If you want to find the secrets of the universe, think in terms of energy, frequency, and vibration.

– Nikola Tesla

It is important to have a basic understanding of energy in the context of spiritual growth. There are many well-written books that describe in great detail what energy is and how it works. Reviewing those details and understanding the science of them may help you further understand and accept this primer. Included below are what I find to be the most important points about energy, which lay the foundation for the concepts that follow. Understanding them without getting consumed by and/or attached to the details will help you understand and integrate the material in subsequent chapters.

Note that slower vibrating energies are often referred to as negative or lower, and faster vibrating energies are often referred to as positive or higher. However, it is really just a matter of where they are *in relation to* each other.

Everything is energy, from the flower in our garden to our physical body to the air we breathe. They are all simply different vibrations. Everything we think, feel, do, see, or dream is energy as well. In fact, there is nothing we can conceive of that is not energy. It doesn't just infuse everything; it *is* everything.

Energy is neither good nor bad; it just is. It is indifferent, simply vibrating at a faster or slower rate depending on how it manifests. A rock has a slower vibration than a bird, which has a slower vibration than a thought, which has a slower vibration than the feeling of love.

Similar energies attract one another. This is the Law of Attraction. Positive energy attracts positive energy and negative energy attracts negative energy. This is especially true with non-physical energies (higher vibrations like thoughts and emotions) where the Law of Attraction operates faster than with physically-embodied energies (slower vibrations like body movement and physical illness). Still, keep in mind that energy is neither good nor bad despite sometimes using the words negative/lower and positive/higher to describe them. They just vibrate at faster or slower rates.

Under this principle of attraction, the energies we radiate—happy, angry, sad, joyful, indifferent, depressed, loving, etc.—attract similar energies into our experience.

Negative energies are stickier than positive energies. When a negative energy meets a negative energy, they stick to one another. When a negative energy meets a positive energy, the negative energy tends to slide past because the positive energy is a higher, smoother vibration and the negative energy doesn't have the resonance to adhere to it. When a positive energy meets a positive energy, there is a resonance between them that reinforces their qualities and helps make them more lasting.

<u>We have an energy body (aura)</u>, a non-physical, electromagnetic duplicate that reflects all our conscious and subconscious thoughts, feelings, emotions, beliefs, perceptions, and physical states. (Note that this book uses the word "subconscious" for both "subconscious" and "unconscious.") It has many layers and some people with certain awakened abilities can see or intuitively read information from it. Our aura expands into our surrounding environment and can be weak or strong, heavy or light, have different colors, different shapes, be dominant or submissive, soft or prickly, etc.

Our physical heart creates a very strong electromagnetic field that pervades our aura. The field is strong enough that it can register in *other* people's brain waves. So, what our heart *feels,* we send out to others, just as we consciously or unconsciously register the heart feelings of others.

The chakra system is the conduit through which energies move from the non-physical to the physical. There are seven major chakras (and many minor ones), each having particular qualities, including associations with specific organs. Each spins clockwise (when viewing a person from the front) and the better the energetic flow through it, the faster its rotation. Our aura reflects the health of our chakras through the speed of their spin. A spiritually evolved person would have all their chakras spinning rapidly and a non-evolved person would have slow-spinning or non-spinning chakras due to their more blocked energy flow. Compromised flow can eventually manifest as physical disease (essentially dis-ease) in areas near or associated with the chakra. Contrary to many sources, chakras cannot spin backwards. If totally blocked, they stop spinning altogether.

<u>Our energy body (aura) is a reflection of both our conscious and subconscious energies</u>. This bears repeating because it is vitally important to what we attract in our life. What is subconscious is not in our mental awareness, and these "forces" nearly always have a more significant impact on what we draw to us than what is in our consciousness. The domination of our subconscious over our conscious energies is the reason we are mystified when we seem to attract the opposite of our conscious intent. It is because the subconscious wields more power. This is the iceberg effect: what is visible (conscious) on the surface is just a small percentage of what is under the surface (subconscious). The stronger, more dominant energies we radiate attract similar forces, which come to be more pervasive in our life. The *external* world that we experience reflects *all* these energies as a perfect mirror of our *inner* world. What we believe, think, want, fear, etc. becomes our reality.

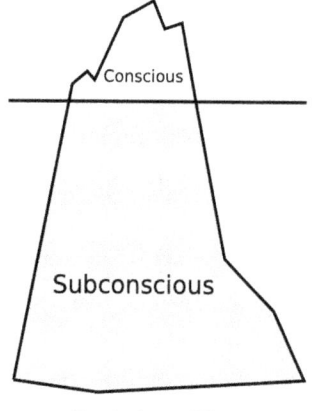

The Iceberg Effect

A Primer on Energy

Our energy body also contains the perfection of our Spirit within, which is our connection to God and our awareness of perfect Truth. When we can consciously align with this highest energy, we increasingly reflect and attract the spiritual ideals to which we aspire.

<u>Subconscious emotions from our belief system drive action from our concrete mind into the physical world</u>. In other words, our conscious, day-to-day habits and manner of living are influenced by our subconscious emotions, which originate from our beliefs. Thoughts, powered by the emotions embedded in these beliefs, create our experiences.

Our belief system is a collection of the thoughts and accompanying emotions of deeply rooted ideas, opinions, positions, views, and judgments. Being mostly subconscious, they are so ingrained in our energy that we are typically not aware of their influence. Our core beliefs are carried in our soul memory from lifetime to lifetime, although our parents, culture, peers, society, workplace, or significant figures in our life can affect them. Often, however, these influencing factors serve to *reinforce* our beliefs rather than change them. When our erroneous beliefs become strong enough that they invite challenging lessons, we can begin to consciously recognize them and take steps to effect changes to our belief system.

Beliefs can have a strong and potentially subversive impact on how we *think* we are living. Since they carry the full creative power of our intent, yet are generally subconscious, they silently infuse our actions without us recognizing their influence, or their power. For example, you may subconsciously fear dogs because one bit you when you were a child, but you may have no conscious memory of it. You may have developed (or reinforced) the belief that dogs are dangerous, which is why you don't like dogs today. The issue can also be viewed on an even deeper level as it could negatively affect your seeing the connection and oneness of all things because you fear and reject another living creature by emotionally perceiving it as dangerous. These kinds of beliefs can inhibit our spiritual growth. Uncovering and observing them for what they are is imperative.

Positive change comes from positive energetic change. We may be able to control our conscious energy and put out more positive vibrations for the universe to reflect, but if our subconscious is working against that conscious intent, we see a minimal effect from those efforts. As best we can, we want to make the subconscious conscious so we can observe and be mindful of *all* our energies. We then have conscious control over what energies we *choose* to radiate (and thus attract) and can make the positive changes we desire. (See *Healing*) Fundamentally, it's a choice. It's always a choice.

Questions:

1. Describe how, when, or where in your life you have felt, seen, or experienced these concepts.
2. How did you feel as you read the chapter? Did it support or challenge your previous understanding of

A Primer on Energy

energy and the aura? Explain any changes in how you now view these ideas.

3. What stood out to you?

4. Wherever you are, choose an object around you to engage with. It can be anything—a table, flower, door, piece of jewelry, lamp, candle, tree, etc. Look deeply at it. What do you see? What do you *feel?* Explore your energetic connection with it and describe.

5. Think of something from your past that you can look back on and know that your reactions and choices at the time were framed by your understanding and emotions of that time. Describe the situation. Does your view of it change after reading the chapter? What changed your thoughts about it?

6. How might you apply any of this material in your life?

~ Chapter 3 ~

Body, Soul & Spirit

Care I for the limb, the thews, the stature, bulk, and big assemblance of a man! Give me the spirit.
– William Shakespeare

Nowhere can man find a quieter or more untroubled retreat than in his own soul.
– Marcus Aurelius

The entirety of our energy can be looked at as being in three parts: the Spirit or Higher Self, the soul, and three bodies (the physical, emotional, and mental). Even though much of what is described below is separated for explanatory purposes, each of the three parts is really a continuum of energy within itself; there is no distinct boundary delineating a lower body from a higher body or a lower energy from a higher energy. Certainly, the lowest of a lower body and the highest of a higher body are so vastly different that they seem almost contradictory, but nonetheless they are on a continuum, a whole characterized by a range of vibrations. Please note, however, that our Higher Self (Spirit) is above even the highest in the ranges of energies, as it is an aspect of God, whose magnitude cannot be quantified. Everything below this perfect inner light is borne out of *our* individual creative power, which, ironically, comes from Spirit. In other words, the power for us to create who we are as personalities (all of our lesser energies) comes from the God within.

Physical Body

The physical body is the outward manifestation of what is occurring energetically in the layers of our auras, which comes from our conscious and subconscious thoughts and emotions. As such, it is not a "cause" but an "effect."

Every one of our physical cells contains the absolute purest energy of perfection, the essence of the divine within. Diseased cells are a manifestation of contaminated thoughts, mostly on a subconscious level. We can restore our diseased cells to health through consciously directed positive intent, shining a light on subconscious issues, and sustained, joyful being. When we *consciously intend* on perfection, that intent resonates with the perfection in our cells and is manifested. (See *Healing*)

We have a thin, auric layer directly surrounding our physical form called the etheric layer or etheric body. It is the first layer of the aura and is the connecting bridge between the physical body and the other auric layers and subtle bodies by way of the chakras. It is included here as part of the physical because it is an exact energetic replica of it. When the physical body dies, the etheric body dissolves.

Chi, or prana, traditionally defined as "life force" or "vital energy," behaves like an electrical system in our etheric body, which affects the health of the underlying physical structures. The easy flow of chi/prana helps keep us physically balanced while a compromised flow, whether underactive or overactive, can leave us energetically misaligned.

Mental Body

We have a lower mental body known as the concrete mind and a higher mental body known as the abstract mind.

The concrete mind is our analytical mind, the part of our thinking that figures things out and processes cause and effect in all situations. It is essentially our brain's consciousness, our logical mind that helps us navigate this three-dimensional world.

The abstract mind is a higher energy than the concrete mind. It doesn't get stuck in analysis but rather *knows* things spontaneously. We can further split the abstract mind into two parts, the lower and the higher. We are conscious of the lower abstract mind when we process something consciously but can't quite grasp its understanding. It is above the analytical grinding away of our left brain's concrete mind. The higher abstract mind is more of an awareness, a knowing. It has a direct connection to divine mind, the creative force of God within us. Ideas and inspiration come through our high abstract mind, although once our concrete mind gets a hold of them, their purity is compromised.

Emotional Body

The emotional body is the realm of ego, glamour, and drama where all our emotions (fear, anger, love, passion, happiness, sadness, jealousy, etc.—both positive and negative) come out to play. It thrives on separation because separation allows comparison, which feeds all manner of fears, inferiorities, and judgments. The lower mental body and the emotional body work together to keep us blind to perfect Truth, with emotions sustaining themselves on lower mental thinking. If our emotional body is active, we are perceiving illusion, as emotions are merely our unique personal reactions to incorrect perceptions, which *always* can be reduced to perceptions of separation.

Emotions are both conscious and subconscious and can greatly define our personality. Do we feel angry, fearful, depressed, unworthy, etc.? Those are the heavier vibrations of the emotional body. More positive emotions like happiness and conditional love ("I'll love you if . . .") are more refined and at the higher end of the emotional body. Conscious or not, emotional energy strongly affects our thinking and is an active component of our belief system.

Because emotions feed on and interact with other emotions (as well as thoughts), ego uses them to perpetuate their existence in their cooperative realm of drama. (See *God & Ego*) A large part of what is known as the astral plane is made up of these emotional energies.

Feeling Nature

Feeling nature is essentially the most refined aspect of our emotional body. As a higher vibration, it is the conduit for the unconditional love, joy, and peace that comes from divine source to feed our Spirit within. It is the knowingness we experience when we just *feel*, deep in our core, beyond the mind and beyond emotions. It is the feeling we can trust, despite what appearances show us. It is a recognition of seeing with eyes of perfect Truth, of seeing things in their proper spiritual context.

Love is experienced through the feeling nature, with unconditional love being its highest level and quality. In fact, it is the energy we are ever drawn to whether we are conscious of it or not. All situations lead us there, some in the form of difficult lessons and some in the form of blissful experiences. Our continuous choosing to keep our energy more in feeling nature and therefore above lower emotions helps us understand and move past the blocks that keep us from remembering our Spirit within.

Soul

The soul registers every action, sound, taste, thought, feeling, and every other experience of every situation we have ever encountered in this life or in any past lives. The collective of all souls is known as the Akashic Records, which is an energetic history of all things experienced on all levels over all time, in the past and yet to come. Our individual soul contains all layers of our perceptions, whether they are conscious or not, including the perspective from the eyes of perfect Truth. It is from this vantage point of Truth that the soul impels us forward on our spiritual path.

Lower energetic aspects of the soul are misperceptions of Truth and contain the memory of negative emotions, thoughts, and actions. Higher aspects are the discernment of these situations in their proper context, seeing them as learning experiences on our path back to remembering our connection with God. The soul records both our error perceptions *and* the perfect Truth of situations, even though we may not be aware of Truth at the time of the experiences.

Our multiple personalities from past and current lives have all their information contained in our one soul, beyond time and cause and effect because time is an illusory concept utilized by mankind. Our soul *is* that collective energy, with all aspects of it accessible if we can tune into its vibration. This includes tapping into past experiences and even future experiences of our personalities from all incarnations.

Since our soul carries all the energy of our perceptions and misperceptions that continue to presently affect us, it is similar to our subconscious. These soul memories continually infuse our life moment by moment, providing us with the choice to either align with Spirit or react with fear as when influenced by the ego. (See *God & Ego*)

Higher Self

The Higher Self is our divine light, the Spirit within, the spark from God that eternally remains intimately and permanently part of us. Because of its purity, the Higher Self is beyond the mental body and emotional body, ever shining its light on everything we experience. It is because of our Higher Self that we can move forward on the spiritual path, as it imbues our soul memory with the unconditional love and perfect Truth of every situation through which we walk. It sees and knows this Truth always and without fail prompts us to remember it. When we ask our Higher Self a question, we *do* receive a true answer, although it can be difficult to discern above the noise of our lower mental and emotional bodies.

Questions:

1. Describe how, when, or where in your life you have encountered these terms and concepts.
2. How did you feel as you read the chapter? Did it support or challenge your previous understanding of the terms and concepts? Explain any changes in how you now view these terms.
3. What stood out to you?
4. Tune into your physical body. What does it feel like? Is it tense, relaxed, stressed, peaceful, reactive, soft, or watery? Find some adjectives to describe it.

5. Ask to experience just your mental body. What are its qualities? Again, find some adjectives to describe it.

6. Ask to experience your emotional body strongly. What emotions come up? Describe the energies? Do they carry power?

7. Picture someone you love before you. Sense their presence. Connect with them heart-to-heart and feel your chest expand with your love for them. Describe the feeling. How does this feeling nature differ from the feeling in the emotional body from Question 6? Did your mental body try to intrude?

8. Choose a notable experience you can remember from a few years ago. What were the physical sensations you experienced at that time? What thoughts did you have? What emotions? Thinking about it now, describe how the passage of time may have changed those physical, mental, and emotional experiences. What has enabled you to see it from a broader context and how do you feel about it now? What did you learn from the situation?

9. How might you apply any of this material in your life?

~ Chapter 4 ~

Three Energies of Being

The universal order and the personal order are nothing but different expressions and manifestations of a common underlying principle.

— Marcus Aurelius

Our manner of being on the earth plane can be broken down into three different energies. These energies are referred to as the "gunas" in the sacred Hindu text, the *Baghavad Gita*, and as the "three energies" in the booklet, *True Detachment*, containing information channeled through Reverend Penny Donovan from the Sacred Garden Fellowship. The three energies can be simply labeled as purity, action, and lethargy, although these words don't adequately describe them. They are our tendencies for *how* we move through life.

1. The first energy is the highest and clearest vibration of the three. Words that describe it are purity, balance, harmony, knowledge, lightness, wisdom, spiritual, centered, understanding, truth, love, unity, and joy. When someone is living primarily from this energy, they are living a spiritual life from those

ideals, truly *being* those ideals. It is the energy of the spiritual seeker.

2. The second energy is slower than the first but faster than the third. Words that describe it are action, passion, ambition, movement, restlessness, attachment, control, greed, striving, lust, recognition, doing, and excitement. Someone living primarily from this energy is always moving and doing, often without much deep reflection of their life. They may accomplish a great deal in the physical plane, but they are limited in their spiritual growth because their busyness has an addictive quality, which distracts from truly being present. (See *Attachment, Addiction & Detachment*) A spiritual aspirant with this energy is constantly seeking new experiences outside of themselves, thinking that the more they do or experience, the more spiritual they are. There is limited seeking within and a desire to *achieve* instead of to *be*.

3. The third energy is the heaviest of the three. Words that describe it are lethargy, ignorance, laziness, inertia, stagnation, indifference, dullness, confusion, carelessness, sluggishness, and delusion. A person living primarily from this energy has no drive to do anything because they would rather believe in being stuck in limitation than try to move beyond it to better themselves. Almost no spiritual growth comes from being in this energy.

Three Energies of Being

Everyone has aspects of all three energies that express from moment to moment, hour to hour, and day to day. We can operate with different ratios of the energies at any given time or period of time. Generally, someone on the spiritual path continues to align more closely with the first energy if they are committed to truly working on themselves and living from the divine within.

When we are in the second or third energies, the angels, teachers, and guides we have around us cannot help because our vibration is too dense. To truly be open to their guidance and assistance, we need to be *willing* to move out of these lower vibrations and into a lighter state of being. Our *intention* to lift ourselves up brings us into the first energy and makes it possible for us to receive their help. (See *Asking for Help*)

Being aware of the three energies is the first step to recognizing when we may be stuck in a vibration that does not serve us. For example, when we begin to consciously catch ourselves in too much action or too much lethargy, we can reframe the situation and view it from a higher perspective. (See *Reframing*) Through our intention to rise above the lower energies, we automatically step into the first energy. This needs to be done for self-transformation. However, it does not mean that we shouldn't look more deeply at what brought us into the lower vibrations in the first place. Doing so can illuminate where our blocks lie. Then we can set a better stage for addressing the issues by being in or intending on moving toward the first energy.

To shift to the first energy, center and intend on opening up to the divine within. Detaching from outcomes and being deliberately present in the moment immediately shifts to the first energy's qualities and thus aligns us with the higher energies to which we aspire. (See *Attachment, Addiction & Detachment*) In addition, meditation, walking in and communing with nature, journaling, connecting with others, and other self-reflective or mindful activities also help encourage and align us to the higher vibration of spiritual growth. (See *Meditation*, *Transforming Baggage*, and *Disconnecting to Connect*)

Questions:

1. Describe how, when, or where in your life you may have felt, seen, or experienced this concept.
2. How did you feel as you read the chapter? Did it support or challenge your previous understanding of different energies of being? Explain any changes in how you now view this concept.
3. What stood out to you?
4. Identify three times when you felt you were in the first energy, the lightest and most pure of the three energies.
5. Identify three times when you felt you were in the second energy of action and ambition.
6. Identify three times when you felt you were in the third energy, the heaviest and most stagnant of the three energies.

Three Energies of Being

7. Which of the three energies do you feel is most natural to you? Is it consistent or do you shift away from it often?

8. What types of thoughts, emotions, and situations shift your energy to the first one of purity?

9. What types of thoughts, emotions, and situations shift your energy to the second one of action?

10. What types of thoughts, emotions, and situations shift your energy to the third one of stagnation?

11. Describe an experience when you shifted your energy from the second one to the first. What triggered the shift?

12. Describe an experience when you shifted your energy from the third one to the first. What triggered the shift?

13. How might you apply any of this material in your life?

~ Chapter 5 ~

God & Ego

God is everywhere. God is as present as the shoes on your feet as He is in the heaven world. There is nothing outside God. Nothing.

– Yeshua (Jesus)

Whenever I climb, I am followed by a dog called 'Ego'.
– Friedrich Nietzsche

God is in everything, ever present. Even the most dreadful thing we can imagine retains an aspect of God, though covered up with the thick, dense energies of separation and protection. There is *nothing* that is not *of* God or *in* God, for God encompasses everything.

Our Higher Self, our Spirit within, is God *in* us, ever expressing divinity. Our Spirit longs to remember our oneness with all-that-is, but it has an adversary in our perception of our *non*-divinity, namely the ego.

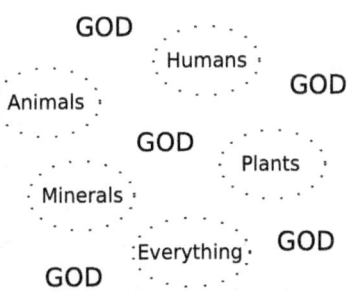

The ego is an aspect of us that uses the lower concrete mind and emotional body to keep us from raising our vibration to know the Spirit within. It works tirelessly toward blocking this connection because, although it is not aware of God, it knows there is something greater than itself that threatens its power. The ego believes that any spiritual growth will be its downfall, so every thought, emotion, and circumstance appears as a life and death struggle.

We created the ego to protect us physically, such as to prevent us from walking off a cliff or walking up to a hungry lion and saying, "Nice kitty." It was solely an instinct for physical survival that gave us the emotion of fear to keep our body safe. The ego, however, has evolved over the ages to create not just that kind of physical fear but emotional and mental fear as well like, "I'm not going to stand for being called a ____!" or "I wonder what my neighbor will think of ____."

Nowadays, ego is the driving force behind emotions and much mental thinking, creating judgments, anxieties, doubts, guilts, and other oppressive emotions. Long ago we needed the alarming voice of the ego to keep our body safe. We have evolved beyond those basic warnings that indicated physical danger to alarms that suggest "threats" to our personalities, making it feel as if we are in harm's way *physically* if we perceive that our *personality* is being challenged or made vulnerable. That is not to say that ego isn't useful when we *are* in physical jeopardy. It is, but its scope of supposed protection has expanded well beyond that primary benefit.

God & Ego

Being one with God, we are perfect creators, and we created the ego through that capacity. So, within us we have a changeless, faultless, all-knowing, all-powerful Spirit within *and* a self-created ego, a loud, dramatic voice with no real substance that crumbles in the face of perfect Truth.

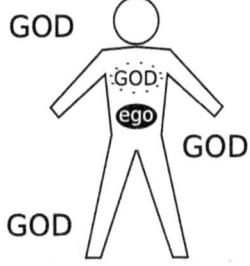

Why *do* we so often allow the ego to dominate our divinity? Because its histrionic shouting demands our attention and we are conditioned to listen more to its higher volume than to the softer but wiser voice of Spirit. Through our continued support of the ego by constantly heeding its voice, we have elevated its guidance and perceived power to a point where we believe that *it* is our God. The more faith we put in our ego, the more it appears to replace our divinity, eventually making us think that *it* is *who we are*.

In our three-dimensional world, ego encourages us to continue to feel separate from others through the illusion of protection. This is enticing and at times useful. However, we need to learn to discern what ego provides that is beneficial versus detrimental to not only our physical safety but also to our spiritual growth. (See *Trust & Discernment*)

How does the ego retain its influence? It directs our attention to something in our soul memory, with its misperceived emotions and thoughts, to show us that we are unsafe. It links that old memory to the current situation and says, "Look at all the bad things that happened the last time you were in a similar predicament!" The alarms bells go off and our emotional and lower mental bodies run wild with fear until we energetically shut off from others, further supporting our separateness. This, essentially, is "sin": authorizing the ego to create or extend the wall of separation, which guides us away from our Higher Self and away from realizing our oneness with all things. What really is ego's protection? It is this wall of judgment and fear, built over lifetimes of feeling that bonding with others is dangerous, of feeling that we are better off fearful and alone because at least *we will survive*. How can we return to oneness when we see the world through the eyes of separation, the eyes of the ego?

Thinking that we can manage our ego by ignoring it, swallowing it, or attacking it head on is to underestimate its cunning. We cannot control or fight it because that just feeds its energy. We can, however, use our *reactions* as a guide to help us uncover what we need to transform. Our reactions point to our dis-ease, and the more we can observe and look at *why* we react as we do, the more we can diminish the ego's influence. The ego does not want us to look too closely because it fears us seeing it for what it is, an empty shell "full of sound and fury, signifying nothing." (*Macbeth*, William Shakespeare)

We can choose not to feed the ego by removing our energy from its reactions and seeing the world from a higher perspective. When we direct our attention (i.e. power) toward supporting our connection with the Spirit within rather than the ego, the ego's influence lessens and we attract that which further supports us on the spiritual path. That is not to say the ego won't find an alternative (and craftier) means of trying to regain its power. Being vigilant to the ego's increasingly complex manners of instigating reactions is an important tool and an ongoing process. At times it may not be easy, but the rewards are many.

The differences between the God within and the ego could not be more contradictory. One *is* God, is created by God, and expresses unconditional love and oneness without even the faintest comprehension of negativity. (See *Seeing from a Higher Context*) The other is created by man, uses fear to protect that which in truth does not need protection (because we are of God), and reinforces only itself to the detriment of its creator and host. God waits patiently in light, beckoning us to remember our divinity while the ego worries and rages like an angry, tormented animal, looking for any excuse to block us from hearing the soft, clear whispers of our Higher Self. The ego knows that there is something greater than itself and fears that power, while God witnesses how we

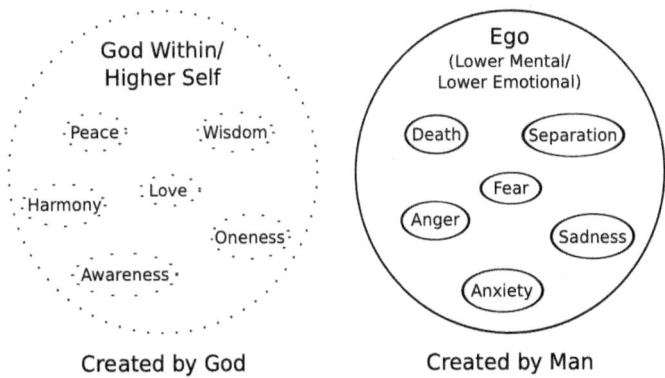

succumb to the ego's voice, yet God allows us our free will to listen to it. (See *Life Contracts & Free Will*)

The following table shows some examples of the ego's thoughts and emotions next to what we would see if viewing them from a higher perspective. Note that *all* the higher perspective views can apply to *each* of ego's defensive reactions.

Ego	Higher Perspective
Fear/anger/anxiety that someone is better than us.	We are all equal and connected in oneness.
Blaming someone for "creating difficulty."	They have brought us a lesson from which to learn and grow.
Feeling offended by someone's judgment of us.	They are in pain and are reflecting our pain.
Being angry with someone.	This shows us where there is a block to our growth.
Feeling hurt by someone's actions.	The behavior is not the person, whom we love.

We have endless opportunities to choose to listen to the voice of our God within over the ego, but the ego is *always* shouting for, or shrewdly seeking, our attention. To live freely and in alignment with God, we must be vigilant in trusting our inner voice and place the ego in

God & Ego

its proper position as subservient to our true power, our divinity. (See *Trust & Discernment*)

Questions:

1. Describe how, when, or where in your life you have felt, seen, or experienced these concepts.

2. How did you feel as you read the chapter? Did it support or challenge your previous understanding of the material? Explain any changes in how you now view these ideas.

3. What stood out to you?

4. Before you started the book, what was your concept of God? How does the description of God in the book differ from your previous understanding of God? Rate on a scale of 1-10 your difficulty in accepting that there is a God within you.

5. How has the book defined or redefined your concept of the ego?

6. Identify an experience from your past where you made a difficult decision. What were the factors influencing the decision? Describe how the God within and your ego may have been in conflict.

7. Identify a past experience where you listened to the soft, knowing voice within over the loud, emotional voice of the ego. How did you feel about the outcome? What made you listen to your Higher Self?

8. How might you apply any of this material in your life?

~ Chapter 6 ~

Healing

Our sorrows and wounds are healed only when we touch them with compassion.

– Buddha

Healing covers a wide range of energies and actions. From prayer and healing thoughts to compassionate words and hugs to hands on manual therapy or surgery, each has its place and each fulfills a purpose.

The physical body is the densest form of our energetic bodies, and any dysfunction of our form is an outpicturing of imperfect mental and emotional states. That is, since we do not see and feel ourselves as perfect (as the divine within us), we therefore must have some imperfection, which manifests in our energetic and physical forms because we radiate (and draw to ourselves) the energy of those imperfections.

For example, someone who is in a stifling marriage where they feel they are controlled and believe that their self-expression has been taken away may eventually develop problems in their throat area. Seeing their aura over time would likely show a graying of that region, the chakra and energetic seat of expression, eventually manifesting in the denser physical body as incidents of laryngitis, thyroid conditions, or even throat cancer.

All healing is an awakening to our inner perfection, a *remembering* of what we have always been. Dis-ease is our perceived limitation made manifest, and healing is the removal of that perceptual blockage through greater self-awareness. In other words, we are healed as we grow spiritually and live our Truth.

A dysfunction in the physical form always has roots in the mind. Under the direction of the ego, we choose (primarily subconsciously) to believe what our lower mind and emotions show us, which is ego's own truth, but not Truth from a higher context. Our erroneous soul memories feed our thoughts and emotions, both conscious and subconscious, stroking our egos and radiating that imperfect energy outwards until it builds into a manifestation of an illness or injury. Even an incident resulting in an acute injury like a broken arm is a representation of a less-than-perfect mindset. If it manifests in the physical body or presents itself as a difficult situation, then we have brought that "lesson" to ourselves in order to open our eyes to see the divine within. The physical body is the "effect"; the energies we radiate are the "cause." Healing the physical body without addressing the aberrant thinking and underlying emotion (the cause) results only in temporary physical healing. This is why making the subconscious conscious is so important. It shines a light into the dark corners of our perceived imperfections, giving us the opportunity to see those erroneous beliefs consciously. It allows us to examine them in the light and consciously choose where we want to direct our energies. Do we want to recognize the light of perfection within or continue to deny who we really are? Denying pushes away the lesson, which eventually comes back in a stronger form in this lifetime or the next.

However, note that even without consciously having a spiritual understanding of healing, people can be wholly healed through complete surrender, belief, trust, love, and/or forgiveness. For example, someone with cancer who believes wholeheartedly that they will be healed on all levels, regardless of how that healing comes to them, *will* be healed.

Concentrating on anything when we are in physical pain can be difficult, and sometimes we need temporary physical healing to bring us to a point where we can begin to understand these lessons more clearly. For instance, trying to contemplate the cause of a lesson while suffering from a debilitating migraine can be challenging without appropriate medication to clear our head. (See *Care of the Physical*) If we truly desire to understand, we must make sure we look at possible reasons *why* the migraine has come to us. The books, *Lessons on Healing* channeled through Reverend Penny Donovan (Sacred Garden Fellowship) and *Heal Your Body* by Louise Hay, offer the psycho-emotional reasons for physical ailments and are wonderful resources for understanding the lesson the physical body is trying to teach us through its injury or illness.

These lessons, otherwise known as healing opportunities, come to us first as whispers, then as pokes, then as shoves, then as a two-by-four to the head. Sometimes we draw to us a major car accident to wake us up to the lesson because we had not become aware of it through the more subtle promptings. Can we become aware enough to recognize the lessons and heal at the first whisper? It certainly would be less traumatic to our physical and energetic forms, but the ego likes its drama and trauma and will pull out those erroneous soul memories to perpetuate its survival and keep us blind to Truth.

When we become conscious of *all* our energies, listen for the whispers, choose wisely, and believe in perfection, we will be healed.

Spiritual Healing

When performing healing on others, it is important to first ask if the person desires a healing. If someone states that they do *not*, we should respect their wishes. Sometimes we may intuitively feel that a verbal "yes" masks their true answer, that they *say* they desire to be healed, but their energy indicates otherwise. If we sense this, we can continue with the healing, knowing that the energy will stay around them until they choose (most often subconsciously) to allow it into their aura to heal.

After asking, it is best to then ground, center, and protect ourselves before beginning. (See *Grounding, Centering & Protecting*) This increases our self-awareness and ensures we don't pick up any unwanted energy from the person being healed. Then we set our intent to heal and raise our vibration through whatever means is most effective, often by thinking of someone we love or connecting with our oneness with others and the natural world. Whatever approach we choose, we want be above our concrete mind and *feel* increasing love and openness within. Then, energetically connecting to the person to be healed, it is simply a matter of picturing them, *feeling* them, as *already* perfectly healed. They are perfect manifestations of the divine, only concealed by the concrete mind's energetic and perceptual mistruths, which express physically. By holding them in light and echoing their perfection through unconditional love, their divine energy is brought forth through the resonance of what *we* put forth. The stronger our focus, intent, and lightness of being, the better channel we are for that resonance of divine energy. The healing goes first to remove the *cause* of any dis-ease and then to where it is needed in the physical body. This is the highest form of healing as it encompasses all other forms and helps to heal the causal misperceptions that created the ailment in the first place.

Methods that heal the physical form without addressing the underlying lesson that brought forth the dis-ease can serve to delay the lesson, which will come again in the same form or another, in this lifetime or another. These methods may be very effective for what they do, but they can be limited to the level on which they operate and are often rooted in details that bring the energy down into our concrete minds. Many energy healing techniques also stress a structure or level within which to work, forcing a mental or other constraint on what otherwise might be a purer healing session. Once we clarify our intent to heal, we need to rise beyond any lower mental body thinking by trusting our intuition and resonating to the open, loving space that fully channels divine energy. Healing ultimately occurs when we release on all levels the mistruths that created and continue to support the dis-ease. Note, however, that when a person absolutely believes they will be healed and willingly releases all the causes of the dis-ease, it doesn't matter what method is used. He or she will be healed.

The recipient also has a role in healing. They can choose to accept the healing or reject it. As noted, while they may verbalize acceptance, their subconscious may reject it. If this happens, know that the healing energy stays around them until they energetically open and let it in, which could be days, weeks, months, years, or lifetimes. Sending healing with genuine intent is *always* beneficial. It is just a matter of when the person being healed chooses to truly and wholly accept it.

Other Healing

True healing is the transformation of a person's negative, imperfect thinking to positive, knowingness of perfection. Because we as human beings are perfect creators and as such can effect this transformation, we can apply the healing technique above to any living thing, including plants and animals.

When desiring to heal non-living places or situations like a country, a business dispute, or an international conflict, healing needs to be sent to the *people* involved, for only they can create the desired change. The exception to this is sending healing to the earth. Because the earth is a living, sacred entity, we can hold her in the light and see her perfection, which calls that light forth. Some healing methods use the earth as a place to send negative energy to be transformed. The earth has had enough traumas and sending negativity to it simply adds to her distress.

Questions:

1. Describe how, when, or where in your life you have felt, seen, or experienced healing as described.

2. How did you feel as you read the chapter? Did it support or challenge your previous understanding of healing? Explain any changes in how you now view healing.

3. What stood out to you?

4. Describe a time when you felt you healed physically, mentally, or emotionally without the benefit of a conventional Western medical intervention. What do you attribute the healing to?

5. Identify a past illness or injury that you feel was needed for you to learn a lesson. What was the illness or injury? What lesson did you learn? Has that lesson repeated itself through other illnesses or injuries?

6. Identify a past illness or injury where you feel that your thinking or emotions during that time contributed to *delaying* being healed. Describe how and why

that could have happened. What thoughts or emotions contributed to the issue?

7. How might you apply any of this material in your life?

~ Chapter 7 ~

Prayer

The function of prayer is not to influence God, but rather to change the nature of the one who prays.

– Soren Kierkegaard

Whether we realize it or not, we all pray. Every time we ask for something to come our way, or obsessively hope it doesn't, we engage in a form of prayer. Do we ever wonder to whom we are really speaking? God? Ourselves? The universe? Yes on all counts.

Prayer that is focused, with uplifting, heart-centered words and feelings that express unconditional love, is tremendously powerful. This is not just saying the prayerful words because we were taught that they were the right words to say, but rather it is deeply felt and known within. This heartfelt prayer nurtures awareness of our inner light and helps it express through us. When we pray to God in this manner, our perfect connection with God is remembered and that which we pray for is invited to us energetically. Whether it is through prayer, affirmations, or meditation, aligning our thoughts, feelings, and words for our highest good cultivates our present moment awareness of who we truly are as divine beings.

Most prayer stems from a want or a feeling of lack, which is rooted in an energy of limitation. Thus, we feel incomplete because we perceive that we don't have something we think we should have. If we feel a *need* to pray for something, then we are furthering a subconscious belief in our imperfection, that our life is not whole without that "something." In truth, God knows we are wholly complete and supports us unceasingly on our path back to realizing God. God sees no lack in us and so cannot conceive of us needing anything. We are perfect in God's eyes, and we are indeed perfect within, but covered up with our humanness.

Our ego wants to stay in control so it mentally or emotionally brings up a dissatisfaction, and we think praying for something to fulfill that perceived lack will help better our circumstances. It won't. We have drawn the situation to ourselves as a learning opportunity and changing the face of it doesn't change the underlying lesson. It is like changing jobs thinking that a different job will make things better, but unless we see and understand the *cause* that is at the root of our frustration and accept the gift of opportunity the lesson brings, we will carry our same mental and emotional baggage to the new job. Before long the lesson will manifest again, creating yet another dissatisfaction, perhaps even a greater one.

Through prayer, we can ask God for anything we desire, but we must let go of the outcome and trust that what God brings is for our highest and best. If we pray for something in the physical plane, setting our intent and *feeling* that we already have that which we desire creates the energetic resonance to bring it to us. (See *Intention & Manifesting*) Through this, we take power away from any issue of lack by not focusing on it, and we turn our creative power toward what we sincerely desire. As with any heartfelt prayer, God provides in whatever form God sees will bring us back to recognizing the divinity within ourselves.

One overarching prayer is praying to God for knowledge, understanding, and wisdom. This helps foster the connection to our Spirit within, our Higher Self that is an undiminished aspect of God.

Questions:

1. Describe how, when, or where in your life you have felt, seen, done, or experienced prayer.

2. How did you feel as you read the chapter? Did it support or challenge your previous understanding of the material? Explain any changes in how you now view prayer.

3. What stood out to you?

4. If you have prayed in the past, why? Do you pray when you feel you have no control over a situation?

5. When praying in the past, to whom were you praying? How would you describe the energy of that prayer

(heartfelt, fulfilling, distracted, lacking, desperate, worried, etc.)?

6. After reading the chapter, how will your prayer change? Take a few moments to pray in the heartfelt manner described. What feels different than before?

7. How might you apply any of this material in your life?

~ Chapter 8 ~

Meditation

Meditation is the dissolution of thoughts in Eternal awareness or Pure consciousness without objectification, knowing without thinking, merging finitude in infinity.

– Voltaire

One of the best ways to connect with our Higher Self (and thus God) is through meditation. We may talk to God through prayer, but God already knows more about us and about what is best for us than we know ourselves. Meditation opens and clears the channel between God and us, providing a direct pipeline to hear and experience God beyond all the noise of everyday existence.

To meditate, we need to rise above the physical five senses, rise above the emotional plane, and rise above the mental plane. Each comes with its own challenges.

To rise above the physical, first we need to be comfortable. No need to contort ourselves into some posture that will have us distracted with pain or discomfort in two minutes. Leave that to the yogis who believe that transcending the physical world means needing to suffer. There is no need to suffer, *ever*. We just get comfortable, focus inward, and feel our five senses withdraw. If possible, we want to sit in a manner that supports our core, allows us to breathe freely, and prevents the inclination fall asleep. If earplugs, a blindfold, candles, music, and incense help, use them. Eventually, additional tools will no longer be needed and their importance as a ritual will fall away.

The emotional body colludes with our mental body to attempt to keep us emotionally charged. When we feel emotions rising, gently and non-judgmentally try to witness them and accept their presence. Instead of reacting *to* them, we can view ourselves as *moving through* them. This can begin to dissipate their distracting grip on our mind. Affirm that we are safe and above any emotions and leave them behind, for now. What arises in the emotional body in meditation can give us insights into understanding the blocks to our spiritual growth.

The mental body also tries to keep us in an endless loop of thoughts, working with the emotional body to steal our focus. We must bring our mental body to stillness, beginning with quieting it down through exercises such as visualizing (and feeling) the serenity of a pond having a perfectly calm, glass-like surface reflecting a cloudless sky. We can use affirmations of peace, but eventually we want to rise above even those to move past the mental body. If thoughts continue to emerge, witness them and let them simply pass by. Like watching movie previews, observe them and then allow them to close naturally so we can get to the main event.

As we rise above the three bodies, the channel to our Higher Self, and thus the conduit to God, becomes clearer. The energy that flows through and around us when meditating calls forth the vibrations that infuse our life with higher energy. Whatever we subsequently encounter will be seen more in alignment with the eyes of perfect Truth than with the eyes of misperception. Sometimes our energy is increased just a small amount, but any increase has an effect on our whole being, and the more we meditate, the more we see changes in ourselves, our circumstances, and our surroundings through the energetic resonance to the higher energy.

Note that there is no bad meditation. Any sitting with intent to raise our vibration helps us along this path, even if we are physically uncomfortable, emotionally charged, and mentally unfocused. Start with a few minutes and increase the time gradually. I encourage you to stay with it. The benefits may be indiscernible at first, but they will soon become more tangible, and before you know it, what may have started as feeling somewhat like a task will be something you are now eager to do.

Guided Meditation

Guided meditation is when a voice or audio recording helps direct us into a meditative space, whether it is for relaxation, raising our energy, attaining a higher consciousness, or for therapeutic purposes. It can be helpful, especially for beginning meditators, because being guided keeps our mental body just active enough to not get too distracted. It gives our mind something to *do*.

Below is a sample guided meditation that cultivates oneness with all that surrounds us. My recommendation is to record the meditation and play it back or have someone read it while you follow along. Focusing on written words while trying to concentrate on what is within can be challenging. Nevertheless, reading this passage can still provide a benefit.

1. Find a safe, peaceful place to sit silently and comfortably with your feet on the floor. Ask your angels and guides to protect and guide you on this journey. Close your eyes. (If you are reading this and doing the meditation at the same time, close your eyes as much as can in order to better *feel* the meditation.)

2. Take a deep breath and slowly breathe out any stress from the day. Take another deep breath, hold it for a few seconds, and release it even more slowly.

3. As you continue to breathe in a relaxing but full manner, feel your physical body discharge any remaining tension. Starting with the etheric layer close to the body, imagine in your mind's eye your aura glowing and extending out about a foot around your form. Try breathing *with* and *through* your aura and feel its presence.

4. Now extend your energy out further so that it fills the room. Breathe. Notice the feeling of fullness as it encompasses everything in the room, picturing this glow all around you permeating every corner.

5. Continue to expand your aura so that it fills the house or building. Feel the connection to the whole structure and everything in it. Breathe.

6. Extend your energy out beyond the house or building to the block, then the neighborhood, then your entire city or town. Breathe in the connection for a few moments.

7. Now expand even further, to your state, then country, then the earth. Rest here for a moment and breathe *with* the earth, feeling her natural power.

8. When ready, extend your energy out into space, first to the solar system, then to the galaxy, and finally to the whole universe. Breathe fully at each step.

9. Reach into every corner of the universe with your energy, knowing that everything that exists is now encompassed within you. *Feel* the oneness with all things, sensing the expansion of the universe within your physical body out into the far reaches of your extended aura. Know that this is who you are and nothing in the physical world can threaten it or take it away. Rest here and breathe with the pulsing of the cosmos.

10. When you are ready, begin to pull back your energy by visualizing your aura receding through space to the earth. Continue to feel the universe within you, as its natural connection is more

tangible now. Breathe again with the earth for a few slow breaths.

11. Continue to bring in your energy, down to the country, the state, the city, the neighborhood, the house or building, the room.

12. Pull your energy inwards from the entirety of the room, extending to about a foot from your physical form, then to about an inch around your body. Despite pulling in your aura, you still retain the feeling of expansion within. In your mind, surround yourself with light and protection.

13. When ready, take a deep breath, wiggle your fingers and toes, and physically feel yourself in your chair. Open your eyes.

Questions:

1. Describe how, when, or where in your life you have felt, seen, done, or experienced meditation.

2. How did you feel as you read the chapter? Did it support or challenge your previous understanding of the material? Explain any changes in how you now view meditation.

3. What stood out to you?

4. How did you feel *during* the guided meditation?

5. How did you feel *after* the guided meditation?

6. How might you apply any of this material in your life?

~ Chapter 9 ~

There Is Only Now

Yesterday is but today's memory, and tomorrow is today's dream.

– Khalil Gibran

We are what we repeatedly do. Excellence then, is not an act, but a habit.

– Aristotle

Every second of the day, we have the opportunity to fully live in the Now. When we are in the present moment, there is no past and no future. All our energy is focused and contained in that instant, resonating with the beingness of all that surrounds us. No thoughts or emotions tug us back to a similar situation from the past, and no anticipation of anything in the future comes to our minds. We are truly being who we are as we were created to be, living solely for the experience of the moment at hand.

Unfortunately, most of us do not have the ability to focus single-mindedly on the present moment most of the time, or at all. But in truth, *we are always in the present moment*. When we remember something, it is a remembrance *in the present moment.* A trip down Memory Lane is actively bringing Memory Lane *to* us so we re-experience it *now* rather than us leaving the moment and going *to* Memory Lane. It is inviting our soul memories to the present so we can re-experience them *now.*

Similarly, thinking of something in the future is really something we are thinking *right now.* Setting goals and planning upcoming events are *current* thinking, as desired outcomes manifest through the energy of our intent *in the present moment.* (See *Intention & Manifesting*)

What can we do to be more focused in the Now? When we observe the present moment as a witness, we begin to see how bringing in past or future thoughts dilute our in-the-moment experiences. We essentially give up a portion of our power to the past and the future, which makes us not fully experience what is around us and within us in the moment. And because we mostly recall past hurts and fears or project future worries, we radiate just those energies we would like to overcome and draw them *to* us instead.

We are *always* in the present moment, which is infinitely powerful and creative. If our power of being in the Now is 100% and we are giving 80% of our attention to the past or future, then 80% of the energy we draw to ourselves will be resonant to those past or future energies and only 20% will be truly experiencing the present. No matter where we direct our attention, *we are still creating at 100%* and that creative energy infuses the experiences we step into tomorrow, which perpetuates the cycle. **What we are <u>now</u>, we continue to be.**

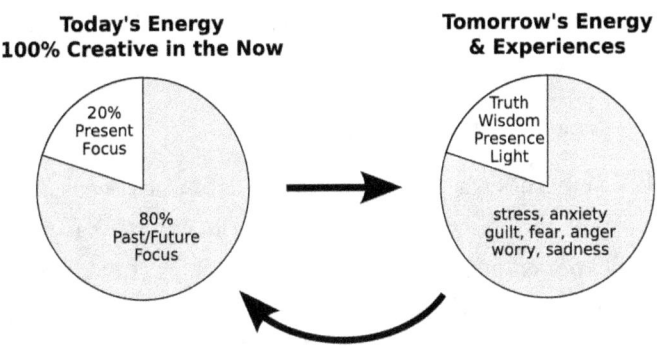

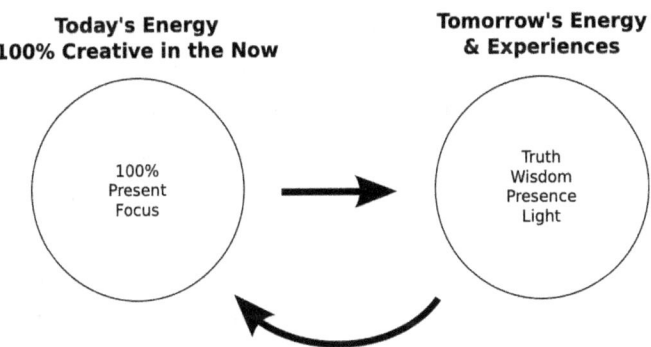

Why not give your full attention and presence to the Now to bring yourself an abundance of enlightened present moments?

Questions:

1. Describe how, when, or where in your life you have felt, seen, or experienced this concept.
2. How did you feel as you read the chapter? Did it support or challenge your previous understanding of

the present moment? Explain any changes in how you now view this idea.

3. What stood out to you?

4. Remember a notable situation from last week. Feel the thoughts and emotions of when you were experiencing it. Knowing that it is not actually happening right now except in your mind and emotions, bring yourself back to the present by identifying and connecting with an object near you.

    Now, think about the past situation again but with a more detached view *from* the present moment, feeling separated from the event by time and space and seeing it as a witness rather than as a participant. Describe how your energy shifts from the past to the present. How does your experience of the past situation change after viewing it in a more detached manner? Can you feel that you create/resurrect the past situation solely in the present?

5. Determine what kind of energy you would like to experience *tomorrow*. Think it, *feel* it, and *be* that energy now and for the rest of the day. If your mind or energy drifts from your intention, gently bring it back. It is important to *feel* that you *are now* the energy you desire to be tomorrow. Now close the book and come back to this exercise tomorrow.

    Describe your experience after you began this exercise. What energy did you feel? How well could you stay in the energy? What are you experiencing today that aligns with your intention from the beginning of the exercise?

6. How might you apply any of this material in your life?

~ Chapter 10 ~

Reincarnation

As a man, casting off worn out garments taketh new ones, so the dweller in the body, entereth into ones that are new.
– Epictetus

Reincarnation is the belief that a person's soul has experienced past lives in other bodies and that we are reborn in a new physical form after death. In truth, past lives, as well as current and future lives, are all being lived simultaneously, since the progression of time is simply a model within which humans perceive cause and effect. Although this can be a difficult concept to digest, in this sense of timelessness, there is no reincarnation. All the influences of past lives are really just energetic resonances occurring in the Now. Our aura carries these emotional echoes of our soul "memories," which influence our subconscious, thereby affecting our belief system and subsequently our concrete actions. However, since we are conditioned to process information in a linear manner, it is easier to use the concept of "past" lives to describe the evolution of our spiritual growth and the development of the lessons we bring to ourselves to move past blocks to increased awareness. So, to understand reincarnation as our three-dimensional brain needs to process it, we need to suspend the above concept of timelessness in order to describe it.

When the physical body dies, our soul memory is carried over into our next incarnation. We leave our old body and decide to enter into a new physical form like we are changing clothes. We just take the baggage of our subconscious with us, namely our soul memory and ego. Unless we become aware of the various aspects of our subconscious and make them conscious while we are in physical form, we will continue to struggle with the same or similar subconscious issues from lifetime to lifetime. Although we choose circumstances in each lifetime that provide the lessons with which to break the subconscious patterns, we will eventually need to *recognize* the lessons when they come and *choose* to learn from them to finally move past them. (See *Life Contracts & Free Will*)

So, why wait? We are *currently* walking through the lessons needed to become more fully aware. We simply need to choose to perceive, listen to, and act on the recurring patterns. And we *will* choose to, in this lifetime or a future one. The most awakened version of ourselves is in us now, awaiting release.

While past lives may have a strong influence on us in this lifetime, remember, they are really all happening at the same time. If we feel an influence and have no logical understanding of why we are feeling it, then it is possible that the energy coming forth originates from a different physical incarnation. For example, why are some people drawn to move to certain areas, have an interest in a particular field of study, or have a natural ability in something that goes beyond their genetic predispositions? These things may be explained by past life influences. Not always, but often.

We can also be acutely triggered by past life energies, often referred to as "bleed-throughs." These are strong emotions, thoughts, and behaviors not created or facilitated by our current lifetime's experiences. There may be a specific place or a particular age that activates a bleed-through to our current life. Someone who physically passed away under the trauma of war on a battlefield a thousand years ago may visit that battleground now and feel heavy emotions as they cross the bridge of time and resonate to their past event there. People have had such experiences on Civil War battlefields. Additionally, someone who passes away under distressing circumstances at a certain age in a past life may have difficulty in this life at that same age because of the resonance to the past life. This is similar to anniversary-related upsetting events just in *this* lifetime, like the death of a loved one. Every year that particular date can recall the associated stress and emotions of the trauma.

However, bleed-through memories don't have to be distressing. When I first saw a picture of Mount Kailash, a sacred mountain in Tibet, I immediately knew I had to go there. I couldn't explain it, but it seemed familiar, and I started planning my trip the following day. Once at the mountain, I had an otherworldly sense of . . . something. It just felt natural to be there, and I was overwhelmed by a lightness of being difficult to describe. Similarly, at Sera

Monastery outside of Lhasa, Tibet (a side trip I planned because of a similar feeling of needing to go there), when I passed under the main gate to enter the grounds, I felt an energy, a powerful resonance that made me dizzy and physically weak. My aura buzzed in a way I had never felt before. Knees wobbling, I continued into the courtyard, feeling confused as the energy vibrated throughout my entire being. At the time I couldn't explain it, but I know now that I was resonating to a past life there. My entire trip was really in response to a bleed-through that connected me to the area.

Another non-traumatic bleed-through is having been deeply in love with someone in a past life and meeting them again in our current incarnation. It becomes an exciting event because of the resonance of love across the ages (in the soul memories). This is often why we feel a natural and deep connection with someone when meeting for the "first time." In contrast, we can also have an intense dislike and aversion to someone if the meeting in a past life was under intense, unfriendly circumstances. Either way, the energy of the past life bleeds through and affects our current life.

So how do we move past these influences? We often don't need to know the details of the past life events to begin to move past their impacts, but we do need to recognize that they may hold a conscious or subconscious energy that feeds our current issues, which impede our spiritual progress. Knowing the details of a past life event *may* shed light on an issue we are working on overcoming by illuminating a source of distress that may have

Reincarnation

previously eluded us. Simply knowing the past life information can provide a release from it, although layers of lessons and issues attached to the experience often require deeper work to fully transform them.

If you seek out information from a past life to move forward spiritually, make sure you are working with a professionally trained and qualified therapist who has an understanding of spirituality and past lives. They can guide you through uncovering and understanding the events that feed the issues you are working on overcoming. It will make for a smoother and more rapid transformation to a lighter energy. (See *Transforming Baggage*)

So, what if the concept of reincarnation still makes you uncomfortable? Perhaps it will help to think of it in the following way. We carry with us early-life experiences from this incarnation, some conscious and many subconscious. These experiences developed into the personality patterns and emotional, mental, and spiritual blocks we have today. We certainly have enough in this lifetime to keep us busy. The belief in past lives simply extends the subconscious source of these current patterns and blocks further "back in time." Either way, we *all* have blocks to our awareness that require transformation if we want to progress personally and spiritually.

Questions:

1. Describe how, when, or where in your life you have felt or experienced the concept of reincarnation.

2. How did you feel as you read the chapter? Did it support or challenge your previous understanding of the material? Explain any changes in how you now view reincarnation.

3. What stood out to you?

4. Identify any talents, natural abilities, desires, or inclinations you have that you feel don't come from genetics, upbringing, family dynamics, social influences, or other "explainable" factors. Examples of this include having a natural musical ability despite non-musical parents and no training or feeling like you were born in the wrong time or place and desire to recreate the culture of that time or move to that place.

5. Describe your connection with each of what you listed in Question 4. How much do you trust in the feeling of having those talents, desires, or abilities? How have they influenced your life?

6. Have you ever felt an intense connection with a specific person or place that defied logic? Describe it. How did you explain it when you experienced it? How do you explain it now? Describe any lessons you've learned from having that experience.

7. How might you apply any of this material in your life?

~ Chapter 11 ~

Perceived Karma

To go from mortal to Buddha, you have to put an end to karma, nurture your awareness, and accept what life brings.
— Bodhidharma

Most people define karma as the grand balancing of the cosmic scales where we bring positive or negative situations to ourselves based on our actions earlier in this life or in previous lives. Based on that definition, we must be mindful of our actions, thoughts, and emotions so we don't draw negative karmic situations going forward in this life or future lives. That is correct . . . only if we *believe* it is.

Karma is only *perceived* karma, an assumption of guilt for our "bad" thoughts, emotions, and actions. When we *think* we need to get even with someone, either because we feel we owe them or are owed something, we create an energy around us that attracts similar energies, which creates a situation that fulfills the karmic law we perceive to be true. And it *is* true, *if* we believe it is. It's a self-validating loop.

If worrying about karma keeps us acting in a more appropriate manner, like not stealing and not treating others with respect, then great! But the worry itself creates an energy that invites anxiety-producing circumstances. It is better to let go of the *perception* that our participation in a situation is good or bad. Life unfolds, and we can simply *experience* it without judgment. This is forgiveness, seeing beyond appearances to release misperceptions that obscure Truth. (See *Fear & Forgiveness*) As we practice forgiveness, appropriate action follows.

What about people who have no conscience, who don't care about the consequences of their actions, or who don't consciously believe in karma and guilt? Subconsciously, any of these individuals may still harbor guilt. Even if their personality in this lifetime does not feel remorse or compassion, they still carry all the information about their actions in their soul memory, which will help shape their next lifetime of lessons. We are all on a path toward recognizing the divine within whether we are aware of it or not. Until the energy of the perceived misdeeds are consciously recognized and forgiven, the guilt remains, albeit buried under the surface of awareness.

Ultimately, believing in karma, whether conscious or not, keeps us spinning on the "wheel of karma" (as Buddhists call it). Until we yank ourselves up out of the fog of this self-perpetuating cycle, we cannot see it for what it is, an archaic perception of personal debt and guilt designed by the ego to trap us unendingly within itself.

Forgiving others and ourselves progressively diminishes our *belief* in karma and helps reduce our creation of additional karma through perceived misdeeds. Then, we can get on with living our life here and now with all the abundance and gratefulness that the present moment brings, always.

Questions:

1. Describe how, when, or where in your life you have felt, seen, or experienced the concept of karma.

2. How did you feel as you read the chapter? Did it support or challenge your previous understanding of the material? Explain any changes in how you now view karma.

3. What stood out to you?

4. Have you ever thought that you were "paying for" something karmically in this lifetime? Describe.

5. Have you ever worried that something you did in this lifetime will come back to haunt you later in this life or another? Describe.

6. Has the concept of karma prevented you from doing something you initially considered doing? What was it? Describe what made you stop.

7. Choose a situation from your past where you made a decision that you continue to feel guilty, angry, or sad about. Did you know better at the time? What made you make the regretful decision then? Describe how your ego may have manipulated you. What have you learned?

Everything I Wanted to Know About Spirituality...

8. How might you apply any of this material in your life?

~ Chapter 12 ~

Life Contracts & Free Will

Life is really simple, but we insist on making it complicated.
— Confucious

When our physical body dies, we transition to a level of existence beyond the limitations of the earth's three dimensions. There, between incarnated lives, we are usually more aware of the limits of the physical world because we are able to experience *being* beyond its heavy vibrations. This is when we have the opportunity to review and further understand our lessons from past incarnations and decide on future ones. Also, we can more easily communicate with our guides, angels, loved ones, and others who have passed over.

We have an increased awareness *most* of the time between lives, but sometimes people pass over with such an attachment to their physical form, to a place, or with such a strong emotion that they bind themselves closer to the physical plane than necessary. During this "time" (for time is still somewhat a factor in our personality that we retain), we begin to choose how and where we want to incarnate again on the earth plane. The mental, emotional, and physical attributes of the parents, physical location on earth, cultural rules, family and friend dynamics, perceived karmic situations, etc. feed into these decisions. We choose the perfect combination of these details to provide what we see as necessary experiences to learn the lessons that help us remember the divine within.

Through this decision process while in spirit, we make "contracts" with others who will assist us on our journey in the lifetime to come, just as we may assist them. These contracts are typically agreements to interact in such a way that will bring opportunities for healing, usually for both participants. For example, the decision to come back to the earth plane is in itself a contract to bring experiences to our family members. We also make contracts with ourselves to experience particular situations or events. For instance, we may plan to be in a certain profession, travel to a particular place, have a yearning to study spirituality, or physically pass away at a specific age in a certain way.

Most important events in our lives are contracted, especially the intense ones that have a lasting impact and from which we learn greatly. Some examples are as follows:

- You contract to become a doctor because you feel you need a lifetime of helping others or to specifically help those who you feel you wronged in a past life and to whom you feel a karmic debt.
- You contract to be born with an illness that leaves you physically helpless your entire life so that your

Life Contracts & Free Will

parents can learn unconditional love, and you can learn to accept being loved.
- You contract to move to another country due to an unresolved issue from a past life in that area.
- You contract to have an angry, aggressive personality to understand the lesson that the energy you radiate comes back to you through angry, frustrating people and experiences.
- You contract to kill another human being to understand the pain in taking another's life or to fulfill a perceived karmic debt, despite the consequences that follow.
- You contract to marry your spouse for the wonderful lessons and opportunities you will provide for each other, whether you stay married or not.

Even though we have contracted agreements with others and ourselves, we can choose to break those contracts through free will and an energetic mutual agreement with the other parties. We *always* have a choice because we can, as perfect creators, create anything, even a change to our contracted experiences. However, because the experiences were planned for a reason—a lesson—if we choose to break a contract, the universe will bring that lesson to us in another way if we have not yet accepted its gift.

Although we have the unconstrained ability to choose, our free will can appear to have "limitations." We may have chosen (contracted) to be born with a strict moral compass, physical weakness, or another attribute that provides a constraint powerful enough to seem to limit our choices. As such, our free will appears restricted. However, even those with such apparent shortcomings can overcome them through sustained and extremely focused will and intent. Helen Keller, who became deaf and blind through an illness at nineteen months old, overcame those seeming limitations to become a world-famous author and lecturer. Australian Nick Vujicic was born without all four limbs and overcame early-life depression to graduate from college and become an internationally known motivational speaker and author. When our will is strong and aligned with divine intent, there is nothing we cannot do or be. With power and guidance flowing through us, life becomes an effortless dance as we relinquish control and limitation and allow our Spirit within to express itself.

Free will also allows us to choose to *not* take advantage of a lesson. We may see an opportunity for moving forward spiritually and consciously choose to go in the opposite direction, away from what we know is better for us. We can also be clouded with fear and other lower emotions that compromise our thinking to the point of not understanding the lesson, and then we choose poorly. Suicide, for example, is a choice almost always made with great fear and hesitation. Although taking one's own life can be a result of a bleed-through resonance to a suicide in a past life, nearly all who pass over in this manner immediately regret their decision. They realize they lost an opportunity for growth while in the physical form. The emotional pain that drove them to suicide may have been contracted to learn how to rise above the pain and not be overwhelmed by it. Even in spirit form, the lesson and the emotional/mental pain remains. They have not escaped it as hoped through the suicide.

We can learn from everything we experience, although sometimes we choose to simply enjoy the experience itself. Contracted or not, there are always opportunities for realizing that we can rise above our misperceptions and see Truth. Our freedom to choose, both in the moment and in what we desire to experience in a lifetime to come through contracted experiences, is how we can grow spiritually. Choosing to see from the Spirit within sheds the layers of limitations that block us to Truth and brings us ever closer to remembering our connection with God, which has always been and always will be completely whole and undivided.

Questions:

1. Describe how, when, or where in your life you have felt, seen, or experienced these concepts.

2. How did you feel as you read the chapter? Did it support or challenge your previous understanding of the material? Explain any changes in how you now view life contracts and free will.

3. What stood out to you?

4. Describe a time in your life when you felt that a situation, interaction, or event you were a part of felt

"contracted." Why do you think so? Did it feel inevitable? Did it change your life's path?

5. Reflect on the reasons why that experience came to you. What were the lessons and have you learned from them?

6. Identify a past experience where you used free will to make a decision you later regretted. What factors influenced your decision? What were you *feeling* before and after?

7. Looking back on it now, what lessons did you learn from that experience? How has it changed how you make decisions?

8. How might you apply any of this material in your life?

~ Chapter 13 ~

Seeing From a Higher Context

The key to growth is the introduction of higher dimensions of consciousness into our awareness.
— Lao Tzu

The universe is change; our life is what our thoughts make it.
— Marcus Aurelius

Increasing our spiritual awareness comes from expanding and clearing the channel to our Higher Self, the aspect of God that has always been within us, just forgotten. We believe, on a sometimes conscious but often deeply subconscious level, that we separated from God and that God is outside us. This is not the case. Our path back to remembering God is through recognizing that this perceived separation is an illusion. When we accept that all things are interrelated and ultimately in oneness, we begin to heal the blocks that obstruct our connection with God. This is not simply a conscious mental exercise. It is also shifting our perceptions on a deep *feeling* level, beyond the concrete mind and emotions. We need to allow our feeling of interconnectedness to transform into a full-blown *belief* so that all our energies radiate a quiet confidence and knowingness. This makes our more enlightened perceptions and reactions natural and spontaneous.

How often do we find ourselves retreating to a safe home base, needing to get to familiar surroundings so we can process some kind of change going on around us? This is not necessarily just a safe physical space but a safe mental and emotional space as well. We retreat to these safe environments (a familiar mindset or habitual emotional reaction) when we feel we can't manage something that is challenging us, so we withdraw to our safe zone to review the situation, whether it is a conscious withdrawal or not.

Because I am blessed (or cursed, depending on how you look at it) with a strong analytical mind, I used my mind as a default response to change. For years, hard, left-brain analysis was my usual method of processing information because it was easier to let my mind overthink a situation than to be in the moment and just experience it. I thought I could exert some control over my surroundings by understanding them with my lower mental body. As I came to explore various spiritual concepts and teachings, I gradually had to let go of scrutinizing the details so I could understand the lessons on a more *feeling* level, just *being* with them. However, my first reaction was always to let my analytical mind slog away at new information in order to categorize, compare, and judge it. That was my safe zone, holding experiences *outside* myself by analyzing them. It was how I perceived I could protect myself. It was not until I realized that this safe zone only served to hinder my *experiencing* life that I began to shift how I processed new situations and information from just *thinking* about them to actively *feeling* them.

Retreating to safety is an innately human response to stimuli seen as dangerous. It is one the ego loves to activate in us. The problem with retreating to a perceived safe zone is that we aren't just withdrawing from the situation, we are withdrawing from life. Life *is* change and change *is* life, and to fear and oppose change is to pull back from the reason we are here, to experience life and to learn and grow from it.

To see and live from a higher context, we must begin to see that change is not threatening, it just is. It is the movement of life around the constant and permanent presence of our Higher Self, our God within. It is seeing and living from the perspective that everything is perfect and was created in love to lead us back to our source, *regardless* of appearances.

One of the greatest challenges of living in this world is understanding that what we see around us reflects what is within us. To be in the flow of life and to move forward through learning our lessons is to use what our world shows us as a tool for transformation. Doing this can be frightening, as we may see characteristics we dislike reflected by others, but utilizing this mirror as an opportunity to grow is a powerful tool for our spiritual progress.

In our fear of change we see and encourage the concept of separation, which must be in us if we are experiencing it around us (the mirror). This perception of separation originated through our belief in duality, which labels one thing good or bad relative to another. If there is no duality, there is no relativity, and therefore no separation.

The yin and yang symbol, for example, is a wonderful depiction of duality, of life. It is white and black (or good and bad, light and dark, hot and cold, etc.) circling each other, ever moving, ever giving and taking. The seed of one can be found in the depths of the other. It is an endless dance of opposites.

In Taoism, it is said that first there was One, then there were Two, then there were Ten Thousand Things. The Ten Thousand Things represent all things in this world, and they stem from the duality of the Two, the yin and yang. But before the Two, there is One, which is beyond duality. The One cannot know relativity, change, or separation because it is above duality, *before* duality. Encompassing all, it is an unchanging, one-pointed knowingness because all things are contained within it. Comparisons and judgments are absent and impossible. This is the oneness spoken about by the sages.

Once the One became Two, the Ten Thousand Things of the world appeared, and we became, and continue to stay, trapped by them, a prison of our own making, entranced by comparisons and frozen with fear of change. We can't seem to move beyond those fears and view life as simply a self-created dance of opposites. When we engage in the dance with a view from the One, we begin to minimize the clutching hold of our judgments. We truly recognize, truly *feel*, that life *is* just a dance party within the duality that we have been trained to see our entire life.

The spiritual freedom we seek cannot be found by grasping at, retreating to, or protecting our perceived safe spaces. Our freedom lies in *remaining open continuously*, not only to life's changes but also to the divine light within us and others. This is our choice. Although often perceived as a weakness, being open and surrendering to the experience of the present moment is our greatest strength. By authentically *living* life in the Now, we submit to divine guidance where we find the freedom to see everything equally and sacred in Truth.

Seeing our life-dance from this higher context helps minimize the grip of our fears and psycho-emotional issues that inhibit our spiritual growth. It can help make the transformation of such issues less traumatic and stressful. (See *Transforming Baggage*)

Questions:

1. Describe how, when, or where in your life you have felt, seen, or experienced this concept.

2. How did you feel as you read the chapter? Did it support or challenge your previous understanding of the material? Explain any changes in how you now view this idea.

3. What stood out to you?

Everything I Wanted to Know About Spirituality...

4. Choose one issue or conflict in your life that you would like to change. Looking *past appearances*, view the issue from a higher context and describe your thoughts. What is the lesson? What do you feel brought that issue or conflict to you? How is it a reflection of energies that are within you now? What have you learned about yourself?

5. How might you apply any of this material in your life?

~ Chapter 14 ~

Transforming Baggage

Look within. Within is the fountain of good, and it will ever bubble up, if thou wilt ever dig.
— Marcus Aurelius

Your task is not to seek for love, but merely to seek and find all the barriers within yourself that you have built against it.
— Jalal ad-Din Muhammad Rumi

We all carry unresolved issues that influence our behaviors . . . our "baggage." Whether the size of a small duffle bag or a large steamer trunk, it inhibits higher levels of spiritual awareness and creates the distorted lenses through which we see the world. We rarely are conscious of the depth or breadth of this baggage, from this lifetime or previous lifetimes, but it colors our perceptions nonetheless.

Our baggage acts like a beacon, inviting energies resonant to what we carry and project out to the world. If we want to lighten our energy, we need to *be* the energy we desire to have around us, a higher energy, so it is drawn to us. When the subconscious dominates the conscious (the iceberg effect), we are unaware of most of the energies we radiate out into the world. If we desire to manifest with more clarity and grow spiritually, we must uncover the mechanisms that keep us bound to our unresolved issues.

To continue to transform ourselves as we travel the spiritual path, we are repeatedly offered opportunities to make the conscious connection from an old dramatic or traumatic event to its current subconscious partner, a hidden dysfunctional pattern of being that inhibits the free flow of consciously-intended energy. Something from the old event colored our perception at the time and we adapted to it, creating a neural and energetic pattern that helped make us feel safe for that time and that age. This coping mechanism was likely reinforced repeatedly, becoming a habitual compensation device rooted in the past event, continuing to "protect" us from similar threats to our ego. We never outgrew the original reaction that now anchors us to responding similarly in comparable situations. A part of us *is* that trapped child who didn't grow up, who refuses to see similar situations from a more adult context.

This dysfunctional, psycho-emotional habit needs to be seen with fresh eyes. When we can make conscious a triggering causal event and see it for what it is—a reaction at the time given who we were and what we knew—we see it from a more mature perspective. The dysfunctional habit was simply built on the misperceptions of youth and inexperience. Recognizing and appreciating this helps knock down the walls that block our awareness.

Transforming Baggage

Our subconscious is similar to our soul memory. What has been recorded in our soul is a combination of Truth (from Spirit) and misperception (from ego), the only two sources that feed it. To begin to perceive more Truth rather than staying stuck in error perceptions, our outdated and misunderstood views of the past must be seen anew with eyes that put these old events into their proper context. These past situations were lessons and opportunities to see clearly, beyond the ego, glamour, and drama that we remember through our emotional and lower mental bodies. This includes thoughts and reactions of anger, fear, sadness, excitement, anxiety, lust, manipulation, greed, and judgment, among others, which are all designed to keep us stuck in perceiving error. When we can see through the errors with newly opened eyes, that is when the correction occurs and Truth is revealed. This is the miracle referred to in *A Course in Miracles*.

For many years I had difficulty making decisions and I could not understand why. Simple choices often felt like life or death. Even easy ones when I was younger, like deciding between chocolate and vanilla ice cream, could be oppressive, and that's without adding strawberry as an option. The biggest struggle was constantly thinking about what I was giving up by choosing one thing over another.

Through several past life readings from skilled intuitives over the years, I received information about certain lifetimes that shed light on this issue. Two past lives in particular revealed that I was commanding many men in battle, and I made decisions that resulted in most or all of my men getting killed. It was not until I was talking about this issue with a trained psycho-spiritual therapist, that I (or rather, we) made the connection from those lifetimes to my current life's difficulty in making decisions. All of a sudden everything came into perspective, and I began to see that my issue was a bleed-through from those lifetimes, my wanting to protect myself and those around me by making the "right" decision. I immediately had a sense of relief and decisions became easier for me going forward. I realized that if I chose vanilla, no one was actually going to die. It seems quite silly on the surface, but such is the grip of the emotional resonance to trauma. I still sometimes hesitate when faced with options, but the visceral fear is no longer present. This revelation solved at least one issue for me; I found I can never go wrong with chocolate . . . unless mint chip is available!

~

Our soul contains the energetic remembrance of any karma we subconsciously *perceive* we need to endure or impose upon another. This perceived karma is part of our baggage and infuses our belief system, which influences our actions on the physical plane. (See *Perceived Karma*) The karmic energy we radiate draws to us those experiences we believe we owe or are owed. Bringing our subconscious thoughts and emotions into our awareness is the first step toward helping us see where we misperceived Truth and acquired guilt when we created the karmic debt in the first place. Once seen, it can be trans-

Transforming Baggage

formed, and we can realize that *there is no karma*. We have taken away its power. We have not done anything wrong, and no one has done anything *to* us. There are no victims and no perpetrators. The ego wants us to believe that *its* dramatic measures can protect us, but the ego is solely interested in self-preservation and so will do anything to keep itself relevant, especially by cultivating and encouraging our perceived karma. When we recognize that karma is simply the ego's unnecessary energy of drama it infuses into our belief system, we can begin to uncover the subconscious blocks that prevent us from moving forward.

To grow spiritually, we need to do what we can to facilitate shining a light on our belief system. It might be through meditation, exercise, seeing a therapist, consciously challenging our fears, reframing how we see situations, interpreting our dreams, observing our thoughts, emotions, and behaviors, going on a pilgrimage, asking for guidance, or a combination of all of them. This self-examination will take patience and practice. At times it will be uncomfortable, painful, frightening, and maddening, but as we progress, the benefits will become clear and far outweigh the struggles. Uncovering our belief system on all levels will force us to see ourselves, *really* see ourselves as we truly are and not as we *think* we are or what we show to the world. This is a bare-knuckled, shameless exposure of our soul to *ourselves*, a staring contest with a mirror that reflects *everything* about us. What do we fear we will see? What will we discover?

When we start to dig, we may find ourselves quickly covered in old, emotional muck. A professional, qualified therapist can be a guide and resource for helping us accept, change, and/or integrate what we uncover. Seeing a trained counselor or psychotherapist as we begin this subconscious archeology, especially a trained, psycho-spiritual counselor, is exceptionally helpful. The importance of finding someone who has a spiritual understanding *and* who has professional psychotherapeutic or counseling training should not be minimized. These traditional methods can be immensely helpful in processing some of the deep, heavy energies that can surface through this work. Intuitive or spiritual "counselors" may have a certain level of spiritual knowledge but, strictly speaking, they may not have professional counseling training which can be invaluable. The same goes for "coaches" who may be skilled at what they do, but who may lack professional therapeutic training. Take care if someone is offering counseling or therapy without proper training and credentials. (See *Discernment with Teachers*)

As a spiritual seeker, transforming our baggage is an extremely important part of traveling the spiritual path. The weight of these mistruths we desire to shed only serve to keep us lower on a ladder that we are all climbing, a ladder of remembering the Truth who we are.

Questions:

1. Describe how, when, or where in your life you have felt, seen, or experienced this concept.

2. How did you feel as you read the chapter? Did it support or challenge your previous understanding of the material? Explain any changes in how you now view this idea.

3. What stood out to you?

4. Observe yourself over a few days and try to notice a habit or knee-jerk reaction you feel you might be doing due to the iceberg effect, that something subconscious is overriding your conscious intent. This might be something that feels as if a decision was being made automatically but if you had time to think about it, you would choose or act differently. Write about what you discover.

5. When and under what circumstances does the habit or reaction occur? What emotions are present? How do you think it sabotages your conscious thinking?

6. How might you apply any of this material in your life?

~ Chapter 15 ~

Asking for Help

A little boy was having difficulty lifting a heavy stone. His father came along just then. Noting the boy's failure, he asked, "Are you using all your strength?"

"Yes, I am," the little boy said impatiently.

"No, you are not," the father answered. "I am right here just waiting, and you haven't asked me to help you."

– Anonymous

As we open up to the idea of all being connected, we begin to realize that we are all in this together and to accept help is to acknowledge this connectedness. If we don't like to ask for or receive help from others, then there will be lessons on our path that will help us recognize that accepting assistance is not something to fear. Life constantly presents us with openings for growth, both joyful and difficult, and it is in the perceived obstacles we encounter that we have the opportunity to see *beyond* the problems. When a difficulty presents itself, there is an energy of the solution contained in it and around it, if we dare to notice. The solution may be in the realm of asking for and accepting help.

There are times for working individually and times when we can use assistance. Use discernment to know the difference. (See *Trust & Discernment*) Be aware that a driving need to work on a problem independently may essentially just create needless suffering. If someone offers us a hammer, would we decline so we could continue to bang a nail with our head, literally or metaphorically?

Our spiritual support team is always around us. Angels, guides, teachers, and others can help guide us through seeing an issue with fresher and wiser eyes, allowing the solution to naturally reveal itself. We can call on any angel, anytime, for help. They are at our disposal and are always willing and able to assist. In fact, even as we think the words of asking for assistance, their energy is already with us. If they cannot come directly, they send one of their helpers, who carries a similar energy of the angel they "work" for. The instant we ask, they are there.

Because we receive the specific help we ask for, we need to be precise with our language such as, "Angels of protection, please protect me from all negative energy as I . . ." or "Angels of teaching, please guide my words during my lecture about . . ." If we request more generalized assistance, like asking for guidance for our highest good as we go through our day, their energy will surround and support us as long as we don't block it by subconsciously putting out an opposing intent. Sometimes we will feel our divine helper's energy around us. Regardless of whether we experience their presence, know they are

Asking for Help

there to help and trust that they assist as best they can and as much as we allow.

Saints or other people no longer in physical form can also provide assistance. Traditionally, Saint Anthony is the finder of lost things so many people pray to him to help locate missing items.

Guides are those in spirit who have lived on the earth plane at one time or another and so have an understanding of what it is like to be in physical form. They can provide practical guidance to help us navigate a problem or issue.

We can also request help from historical or fictional figures. For example, we can call on Albert Einstein if we could use assistance from his powerful brain. Superman and other superheroes have energies that reflect their particular powers. These thought-forms have been infused by the awareness of millions who know their stories, despite them being fictional. When we tune into them with intent, we draw to us the specific resources we ask for to help us with our difficulty. Whomever we are drawn to think of, we can call on them for support and assistance. If they cannot come, someone who might even be a more suitable partner for our situation will arrive.

Asking for help for our highest and best ensures the presence of the highest energies and most appropriate circumstances for our given situation. There is no limit to the information and guidance we can request. Note that we want to use discernment to identify which lessons we need to manage *ourselves* because those lessons are *our* responsibility. However, others (both incarnate and discarnate beings) can support us as we navigate through those challenges.

Finally and most importantly, we can ask our own Higher Self for help. Since we are tuning into the divine within, the answers come from Truth, which helps us see both the problem and solution more clearly. As we ask to be made aware of what needs to be done on the three-dimensional level to resolve the issue, our openness invites what appropriate actions to take.

All guidance is available to us. Simply ask . . . and receive.

Questions:

1. Describe how, when, or where in your life you have felt, seen, or experienced this concept.
2. How did you feel as you read the chapter? Did it support or challenge your previous understanding of the material? Explain any changes in how you now view asking for help.
3. What stood out to you?
4. Have you ever prayed for non-physical assistance at a time of need? Describe.
5. Have you ever *felt* a non-physical presence at a time of need? Describe.
6. Describe a current problem you feel troubled by.

Asking for Help

7. Close your eyes and take a few slow, deep breaths. Imagine the energy of the problem contained in a form, like in a box, bag, or other shape you feel drawn to use. Now ask for assistance in finding a solution to the problem. With your eyes still closed, look around the problem-form. What do you see? What do you feel? What solutions present themselves, if any? Describe your experience with this exercise.

8. How might you apply any of this material in your life?

~ Chapter 16 ~

Reframing

My life has been filled with terrible misfortunes, most of which have never happened.

– Mark Twain

Picture yourself driving down the street in the morning and someone swerves in front of you causing you to slam on the brakes, but no contact is made. How do you feel? Are you angry?

Now you see it is some teenager who is texting while driving. How do you feel now? Does that make you even angrier? You might ride their bumper for a while to show them how you feel. Your frustration leads you to think, "Who are they to do that to me!?" You might arrive at your workplace and share what happened with your colleagues, showcasing and justifying your anger to others who you know would understand. Getting others to agree with your reactions makes it right, right? You might take the angry emotion home with you at the end of the day, continuing to stew and steam about it, causing your partner, children, or neighbor to ask what's wrong. Your prolonged agitation makes you react angrily.

Now let's redo the story. You get cut off on the road and have to slam on the brakes. After a quick anger washes through you and an expletive escapes from your lips, you notice it's your neighbor's car. You remember they are very pregnant and are due today! You realize they are likely speeding to the hospital to have their baby. How do you feel about being cut off now? Happy for them? Guilty for being angry and judging them?

In both scenarios, to an outside observer, the exact same thing happened. You got cut off, no contact was made, and no one got hurt. To you, however, your emotional reactions were likely on opposite sides of the spectrum. Which would you prefer to carry around all day?

When we experience an emotion, that emotion can stick with us for seconds, minutes, hours, days, weeks, or longer. By consciously observing our reactions to situations, we can begin to shorten and even eventually eliminate carrying around the negative emotions that reinforce the past issues we are working to eradicate.

With the first situation above, we may wake up the next day still thinking about it and feeling angry. The flash of fear brought on by the perceived danger of a possible accident set our ego on fire. If we can *consciously notice* our emotion, we can *choose* to reframe it by seeing it for what it was. A car cut us off. That's all. Ego's attachment to the drama wants to make it a bigger deal than it is and trap us in additional karma. (See *Perceived Karma*) The person who cut us off probably isn't thinking about the near miss, and even if they are feeling guilty about it,

Reframing

the only thing we can do to help the situation is to forgive them, which helps dissipate both their and our emotions. (See *Fear & Forgiveness*)

Once we start noticing and reframing, the next time a similar situation happens, we may only carry the emotion for a few hours before observing it consciously, reframing it for what it truly is, and releasing it. Then the next time it might be just a few minutes before we release it, then a few seconds. With practice, we become mindful of the emotion as it rises up and are able to release it before it fully forms, thereby lessening its impact. The idea is to eventually be totally mindful in the moment so the negative reaction doesn't even begin to form.

We can apply this reframing to any situation, especially to those that cause fear, anger, or anxiety. We can constantly observe and reframe until we develop the reflexive habit of seeing the emotions coming and then can spontaneously and immediately rise above them. This shifts our overall energy upwards by reinforcing to our belief system that those negative reactions are incongruent with our interconnectedness with others. Those emotions, which are rooted in subconscious and archaic belief systems, are obstacles that inhibit the flow of our internal divine energy. Reframe, and take a big step toward healing and awakening.

Questions:

1. Describe how, when, or where in your life you have felt, seen, or experienced this concept.

2. How did you feel as you read the chapter? Did it support or challenge your previous understanding of the material? Explain any changes in how you now view reframing.

3. What stood out to you?

4. Select a situation from your past when you became angry. Why did the situation trigger your anger? Describe and explain.

5. Was there another way for you to view the situation as it occurred? Is there another way to view it now in retrospect? Describe.

6. If it was a personal attack, did you invite it because of your anger at the person? If it was an accident, can you see it from the other's perspective?

7. How do you view *your* emotions in this? What drama is your ego whipping up?

8. Describe another way of handling the situation by reframing the situation from a higher context.

9. How might you apply any of this material in your life?

~ Chapter 17 ~

Grounding, Centering & Protecting

Keep your eyes on the stars and your feet on the ground.
— Theodore Roosevelt

I want you to be everything that's you, deep at the center of your being.

— Confucius

Grounding

Grounding is a process of feeling a connection with Mother Earth. When we are *un*grounded, our energetic center is concentrated and more dominant above the waist, we are more scattered, and we don't feel as connected to the physical plane. Essentially, we are skating on a surface above the earth, not truly feeling and appreciating her wonders.

One way to ground yourself is to make sure your feet are on the floor, or even better, your bare feet are directly on the grass or dirt outside. Imagine roots coming out of your feet and going deep into the earth. Feel the connection and the earthly energy coming up through the roots into your feet, up through your legs, and radiating throughout your body. *Feel* it and stay in that feeling for as long as you desire and are able, but longer if you have been feeling particularly ungrounded. To close this exercise, pull your energetic roots back up into your feet and thank the earth for all that she provides.

Centering

To be centered is to be at home within ourselves. It is to nurture the knowing and feeling of our Spirit and foster our connection with other living beings. We are centered when we see and feel our proper place in any situation and see with the eyes of Truth, the eyes of the Spirit within.

An ongoing meditation practice strengthens our feeling of being centered because it helps us connect with our Higher Self through shedding our layers of misperceptions and unawareness. Centering is essentially a quick meditation that brings our conscious awareness and energy in line with our heart, rooting us in love and compassion. This enables us to see and experience everything around us from that higher perspective, from a more spiritual and connected context.

To center, take a few deep breaths and relax your body. Focus on your heart-space, feeling love and compassion for yourself, and then extend that love to others. Feel and know the Spirit within and know that you are safe and that anything (or anyone) that presents itself to you in the earth plane is doing so for your highest good. *Feel* it. Be sure to protect your aura after centering. (See *Protecting* below)

It is important to note that while grounding and centering are similar, they have different functions. Grounding reinforces our connection with Mother Earth with respect to the earth plane, while centering stirs the remembrance of our everlasting connection with Spirit and our oneness with others. Both are important for being present in the Now and connecting with the flow of life. Repeated practice will help lighten our energy and break down blocks to our spiritual growth. (See *Transforming Baggage*)

Protecting

Protecting ourselves from the mental and emotional energies surrounding us is an important practice. There are three fundamental ways we can do this: by staying in a positive, lighter, and more loving space, which causes negative energies to slide past us; by actively intending, visualizing, and feeling (and thereby creating) a layer of "armor" around our aura; and by asking for help from angels and guides who specialize in protection.

Our personal energetic fields, our auras, interact with those of other living things. Keeping our energy as high as we can through joyful, connected, and loving thoughts sustains a purer vibration, creating a slippery energetic shield that naturally minimizes the absorption of heavier energies. (See *A Primer on Energy*) This is a manner of *being* in a loving and compassionate space where our aura is too refined for the lower energies to penetrate. Like trying to pour gravel through a sieve, the negative vibrations (the gravel) can't pass through the sieve (our slippery aura) because they are too dense.

Another way to energetically protect ourselves is to intend on putting an etheric shield around our aura. (See *Intention & Manifesting*) To do so, imagine and feel our aura's multiple layers extending around us, just as they naturally do. Now draw these energies inwards toward our physical form on all sides, feeling the aura condense as we bring it very close to our body. We can also imagine any lower vibrations in our aura being expelled as we do this. Stay with this "compacted" feeling for a few moments, reinforcing our intent to keep the aura close. Next, add a protective shell of a material around the outside of the aura. Different types of coverings function differently, but each layer can be beneficial. Some examples are below:

- White light – This has a purity, resonant to divine light, that is powerfully protective and prevents negative energies from affecting us. It also can be a beacon to all sorts of energies as many beings—both physical and non-physical, positive and negative—are drawn to its brightness. Keeping our energy positive and loving naturally raises our vibration closer to this white light of protection.
- Blackness – This has the effect of making us energetically invisible. If we want to reduce the likelihood of someone noticing our energy as we pass by, this is good to use. Note that we should not use this

Grounding, Centering & Protecting

when in a vehicle as it can reduce our visibility to others and increase the chances of an accident.
- Armor – As you might think, projecting armor around our aura shields us energetically. The type and quality of the armor we choose reflects the level of protection it provides.
- Mirrors – Putting mirrors around our aura reflects whatever energy coming to us back at itself. The idea is that, for example, a negative, heavier energy sees itself and is frightened, and so leaves us alone.
- Spikes – Visualizing spiked projections on the outside of our aura serves to deter energies from approaching, which could have unintended consequences to those with whom we are close. We would present ourselves as having a "prickly" aura.

A third way to protect ourselves is to ask for help. Calling on angels of protection can immediately bring their powerful energy to us for assistance in creating and sustaining a shield to guard against unwanted energies. Setting our intent and stating clearly what we desire produces the requested effect. (See *Asking for Help*)

Whatever type of protection we can think of and focus on with intent, we can create. Religious, mythological, and superhero symbols carry the energy of belief of many people, so they already have a power to them. Something deeply personal can have an emotional power that helps focus and fuel our intent. Whatever we find useful provides protection when created with clear, focused, and sustained intent and when projected with a *knowingness* of safety, absent of fear.

When we are not protected well, we can be psycho-energetic sponges to the energies around us, taking them on to such an extent that they subconsciously affect our thoughts and behaviors. But others' energies are not ours to wear, and we give our power away by allowing them to influence us. This is similar to our calling forth our own soul memories into the present moment, which gives creative power to them. Why give our power away for someone else's lower, energetic causes?

The effects of taking on others' energies can manifest subtly, and we may not recognize that a change in what we are thinking or feeling is not really our own. When loving, centered, grounded, and protected, we stand in a place where we know more clearly who we are and can better see the Truth of the situation before us and our place within it. Consequently, it is much easier to know which thoughts and emotions are *not* ours. We may think and feel *others'* thoughts and emotions, but as we practice and develop our discernment, we gain awareness and learn to differentiate between their energies and ours. This is how psychics and intuitives can "read" people. Through their protected energetic space, they can consciously distinguish between their own energies and those of the person they are reading.

As spiritual seekers, we are not yet able to *completely* shield ourselves from the energies around us, so some do stick, often because of a resonance to a belief held in *our* aura, whether conscious or subconscious. There are lessons to be learned in this, as our environment is reflecting that aspect of ourselves back to us so we can more clearly see how that issue is a part of us and affects our life.

Having a daily practice of centering and protecting is helpful toward minimizing acquiring and carrying the energies of others. Consequently, we are more genuinely our own selves, feeling and radiating who we are exclusively, without being confused by blending in additional energies that are not ours. We certainly have enough of our own to work with.

In addition to a daily practice, we can reinforce our aura by centering and protecting again before entering difficult situations. Accordingly, we enter those situations as our true selves and are less prone to being adversely affected by the energies of the people or place.

Having a protected aura helps us be with only *our own* energies, which supports our *being* truly ourselves. Whether we protect by naturally being in a higher, more loving energetic state, by intending on shielding ourselves from the energies around us, or by asking for help, protecting our aura is a vitally important and effective tool for our spiritual growth.

Questions:

1. Describe how, when, or where in your life you have felt, seen, or experienced these concepts.

2. How did you feel as you read the chapter? Did it support or challenge your previous understanding of

the material? Explain any changes in how you now view grounding, centering, and protecting.

3. What stood out to you?

4. Use the description in the chapter to practice **grounding**. How does it feel during and afterwards?

5. Use the description in the chapter to practice **centering**. How does it feel during and afterwards?

6. How does the feeling of grounding differ from the feeling of centering?

7. Use the description in the chapter to practice **protecting**. How does it feel during and afterwards?

8. Ground, center, and protect in the morning and come back to this exercise at the end of the day. If you feel you need to ground, center, and/or protect again during the day, go ahead.

    How did the exercises affect your day? Describe the differences between this day and a regular day when you haven't done any grounding, centering, or protecting. Include differences in energy, focus, mood, etc.

9. How might you apply any of this material in your life?

~ Chapter 18 ~

Intention & Manifesting

The best way to predict your future is to create it.
— Abraham Lincoln

Our life is what our thoughts make it.
— Marcus Aurelius

As a function of the divine within, we create continuously and as such, are perfect manifesters. *We precisely and unerringly manifest our combined conscious and subconscious energies.* The more time and attention we devote to something (conscious or subconscious), the more we power our manifesting intent to create it in this three-dimensional world.

The outcome of our manifesting can be witnessed all around us. If we start a project and it fails, then something in us manifested that failure as a lesson. Was it doubt in our skills, fear of success, or something else rooted in that long-ago event from childhood when someone said we would never succeed at anything? You name it. Something pulled the oar in the opposite direction of our conscious desire.

Intent is the energy that focuses and holds our desire in place. Staying centered with our intent requires practice, and in most cases, lots of practice. Our multitasking culture inhibits one hundred percent focus on just one idea, let alone sustained concentration, yet that is the very thing that creates the manifestation of our desires. Spreading our focus dilutes the energy of the intent and compromises the process of manifesting. A split mind does not fulfill our desires but rather creates the *expression* of the split mind. That is, we manifest in our lives as our thoughts are . . . divided, distracted, and with minimal depth, and then we wonder why we don't have what we want.

Some of this disharmony expresses as tension in the physical body because energetically, we cannot reconcile the division in our mind. If we choose one thing, we feel guilty for *not* choosing the other, and vice versa, or we are uncertain that we would enjoy either choice. Either way, our physical and energetic bodies hold the conflict.

So how do we move beyond these blocks? When we focus on one project, task, or desire and do so *without fear and doubt*, we are in our abstract mind, the higher vibratory part of the mental body that is linked with divine mind. (See *Body, Soul & Spirit*) In that space, we are unbounded and limitless in our creative abilities, and the power of creation is ours. Once our analytical, concrete mind sneaks into our thoughts with next steps—trying to process what we are thinking—doubts, details, and "what-if" scenarios arise and our pure and focused intent becomes compromised.

This is why to manifest we need to *feel* and *know* that we *already* have what we desire. This feeling and knowingness energetically bypasses the lower mental body and emotional body and taps into the unlimited and boundless creative energies of the infinite potential of God through divine mind. When we feel and know the resonance of/to that limitless energy, we become a channel for it to create *through* us.

Feelings and emotions have the power of our belief system, so they are stronger than thoughts alone, which can become diluted or dissipate quickly. When we truly *feel* something, the energy of that feeling pervades our physical and auric bodies, powering and directing our intent. Our belief system has such manifesting strength because it carries the unceasing, inspired strength of our feelings and emotions, continuously infusing all subsequent actions, thoughts, and emotions, often without us being consciously aware of their influence. This is why we want to release our belief system's negative, limiting aspects and reinforce the positive. Since our belief system operates constantly in the background of our lives (as our "faith"—what we believe in), it carries the significant manifesting power to create *itself* in the form of circumstances and energies that are a direct reflection of it. Its energies project outward and are collectively reflected in our surroundings, people, pets, places, situations, etc. Making conscious the subconscious beliefs that do not serve our highest good is absolutely necessary for understanding why we create the circumstances that continue to vex us. As these beliefs become conscious, we gain the opportunity to choose a better path for ourselves and then can consciously release the old, dysfunctionally-patterned thoughts and emotions. The subconscious is the realm that we can decode to improve our conscious intent and manifesting power, and thus our movement along the spiritual path. (See *Transforming Baggage*)

We can set our intent by feeling and knowing what we desire. Often, however, we get stuck on the *outcome* of a desire, situation, or event by imagining a *specific* result and believe that we must have *that* result to satisfy us. This creates an attachment to the outcome that blocks our divine energy from expressing its full, creative, manifesting power. Thus, our clutching to results undermines our intentions. (See *Attachment, Addiction & Detachment*)

The fuel, so to speak, to power this manifesting energy could best be described as enthusiasm. The joy and excitement of knowing that we already have what we desire, whether we yet observe it in this three-dimensional world or not, provides the ongoing energy to create the circumstances that bring those desires to us. When we bring enthusiasm to our intent, feeling, and knowingness, we *do* manifest as we wish.

This book is an example of manifestation of intent. I knew I wanted to share what I had learned over my many years of study but didn't know how or through what medium it would happen. I had a feeling of *knowing* that I would express it in some manner, which created the energy that influenced me to sit down one day to write a chapter. From there, my enthusiasm grew and many months later, I found I had written all that I had wanted to originally express. Not surprisingly, during the process when I was *thinking* too much, the writing became difficult. Conversely, when I was *feeling, trusting,* and *being* in the flow, the words came effortlessly. Such is our energy and how we can use it to manifest our desires. When we can trust our intent by letting go of specific outcomes and allow ourselves to be guided, divine inspiration flows to us and through us.

Stay focused, stay centered, stay clear, be enthusiastic, and *feel* and *know* that you already have what you desire.

Questions:

1. Describe how, when, or where in your life you have felt, seen, or experienced these concepts.

2. How did you feel as you read the chapter? Did it support or challenge your previous understanding of the material? Explain any changes in how you now view intention and manifesting.

3. What stood out to you?

4. Set an intention to manifest something relatively small or trivial that you can easily visualize and connect to. An example would be choosing to see a particular make and color of a car within a day. Describe what it is and then state it as if it has already happened, like "I am seeing _____ in my life today."

5. Re-read your statement and note how it *feels*. Do you have a *knowingness* that it is happening or are you just saying the words? Gauge your *belief* in what you are intending.

6. If you don't fully believe your intention, consider using some of the concepts described in previous chapters: being in the Now, asking for help, grounding and centering, shifting to the first of the three energies, seeing from a higher context, or reframing. Re-read your statement after using one of more of these concepts and be *excited* at the prospect of manifesting it. Which concepts did you use? How does it *feel* now? Describe your level of belief in the intention.

7. Repeat the intention over the time period you indicated using any of the concepts you are drawn to use. At the end of the time period, evaluate your success at manifesting the intention. How did you do? How did you *feel* throughout the process? What got in the way psychologically or emotionally? Explain.

8. How might you apply any of this material in your life?

~ Chapter 19 ~

I AM & Affirmations

I am as bad as the worst, but, thank God, I am as good as the best.

– Walt Whitman

"I am . . ." is one of the most powerful statements we can make. As creators in the present moment, "I am . . ." sets the stage for the creation of what follows. When we say, "I am sick" or "I am tired," we energetically reinforce that condition. And when we say, "I am loved," "I am healed," or "I am light," we reinforce our intrinsic Truth, light, and perfection. Which do you think is better?

Obviously, positive affirmations are more beneficial than negative ones, but either will reinforce its energy in our belief system. Stating or thinking, "I am a good friend," "I am smart," or "I am loving" strengthens the positive attributes in our subconscious mind, while "I am stupid," "I am unworthy," or "I am afraid" supports the negative qualities.

Similarly, using "my" when talking about negative conditions such as "My head hurts" or "I hate my job" professes ownership of the negative condition. If we absolutely need to verbally express a negative condition, using "the" instead of "my" can reduce the energetic resonance of the thoughts and words because "the" states that it exists and could be a passing phase while "my" claims it as our own.

We can create an affirmation about anything, but keep in mind the creative power of it. Choosing knowledge, wisdom, and understanding or choosing to see the Truth of a situation takes us further spiritually than affirming our talent at something physical like "I am going to win the game!" although that carries power as well. Sometimes we need to start by affirming more tangible, worldly things to feel the effect of our I AM power. Nevertheless, continually affirming the tangible keeps us stuck in three-dimensional thinking. To enhance our spiritual growth, the physical world needs to be seen from a higher context.

On its own, "I AM" is the ultimate affirmation of who we are, our Spirit within, our beingness, for it strips away all the distracting three-dimensional thoughts, emotions, and physical conditions that cover our inner light. When we can step back and begin to observe that we are not our thoughts, not our emotions, and not our physical form or its conditions, we eventually come to the realization that simply, I AM. We can live from this natural state if we can but simply *remember* and *feel* it.

As an exercise, find a quiet place to sit comfortably. Allow the body to relax. Breathe deeply, expelling the stress of the day. Now think of an issue that is troubling you. Affirm, "I am more than this situation about

_____." Breathe fully, repeating the affirmation softly in your head.

Now affirm, "I am more than this body." Breathe, knowing you are greater than your physical form.

Next affirm, "I am more than these emotions." Breathe out any heavy, negative emotions so that only the positive feelings remain.

Then affirm, "I am more than these thoughts." Feel your mind release its hold on your thinking as you breathe out the clutching of the lower concrete mind.

Next affirm, "I am peace," and notice the feeling that pervades your aura. Sit with this energy of peace.

Then affirm, "I am light," and visualize your body and aura increasing in brightness as your divine light within expands as you repeat it. Breathe deeply but naturally, allowing this light to grow on the in-breath and expelling anything not of light on the out-breath. Do this for at least a minute. When full, bring in your aura to protect your increased peace and light.

Did you notice any difference in feeling with the affirmations? How prominent is the issue that was troubling you now?

The power of affirmations is ours. We can affirm anything that will help raise us up and out of the issues that we perceive hold us back from being the spiritual being that we are.

Questions:

1. Describe how, when, or where in your life you have felt, seen, or experienced these concepts.

2. How did you feel as you read the chapter? Did it support or challenge your previous understanding of the material? Explain any changes in how you now view I AM and affirmations.

3. What stood out to you?

4. Do the exercise at the end of the chapter. Did you notice any differences in feeling with the different "I am . . ." affirmations? Describe.

5. Describe any differences in how you viewed the issue that was troubling you from before the exercise to after. How prominent is it now?

6. How might you apply any of this material in your life?

~ Chapter 20 ~

Trust & Discernment

As soon as you trust yourself, you will know how to live.
— Johann Wolfgang von Goethe

All I have seen teaches me to trust the creator for all I have not seen.
— Ralph Waldo Emerson

Trust is a huge and quite common lesson on the spiritual path. We are challenged to trust all the time; our spiritual teachers, our intuition over the voice of our ego, our lessons and opportunities, that which is happening is for our highest good, etc. The overabundance of stimuli in our multitasking lives constantly begs us to listen to what is outside us—the clamor, drama, and glamour—instead of the quiet voice within. How can we focus on ourselves when we are energetically prodded by such things as the dirty dishes in the sink, our overloaded email inbox, office gossip, our emotional reaction to the sensationalized news, work and family obligations, and all the tasks and chores of the day we haven't yet completed? How do we trust that this quiet voice of our inner light speaks to our best interests better than the distracting noise around us?

We can't, unless we begin to believe it does. We must take a leap of faith to *begin* to trust, and then the positive feedback of the feeling that we chose to listen to the right voice makes itself apparent. It is made clear through a soft knowingness within, an openness felt in the solar plexus and heart.

When we trust, we open the doors to all kinds of help. Solutions more readily present themselves and angels and guides can more easily communicate what we need to hear because we have opened our energy to invite in the necessary information for transformation of the issue at hand.

Not trusting makes us feel we need to control the situation. If we cannot believe that what is happening around us is for our highest good, then the ego is controlling the situation for its own ends, which perpetuates the lack of trust. This blocks the allowing and openness that helps us live from our Truth in the Now. Trust allows. Not trusting obstructs.

Trusting also fosters appropriate discernment, the ability to listen to, recognize, and respond from that feeling within more than from the perspective of what appearances show us with our physical eyes. We begin to hear and act through *feeling* the energetic whispers of the lessons so we don't get the two-by-four to the head that knocks us down mentally, emotionally, and/or physically. Discernment is trust put into practice.

Trust & Discernment

Trusting in our inner voice over the multiple outer voices or the voice of the ego is a challenge because our culture today stresses the importance of appearances over the feelings of Truth. But it is just those appearances that provide the lessons through which we can begin to recognize our imperfections and miscreations. These lessons most often come in the form of perceived challenges. Learning to instinctively trust and discern through actively *practicing* trust and discernment goes a long way toward helping us see with more clarity and drawing to us the energies we need to move past our misperceptions. Having confidence in ourselves and our ability to rise above our circumstances feeds the trusting of our inner voice. Even faking confidence puts us in a state of confidence. So, when we feel challenged to trust, we need to get confident, even if it feels forced, and trust follows.

Of course, we must not forget to use our increasing powers of discernment to avoid potentially dangerous situations. We don't want to force trust when it is counter to our intuition. Know that when intuition informs us about danger, no *emotion* is present, just a quiet *knowing* of what action or non-action to take, and a path unfolds.

When I worked as an analyst, everything appeared to be going well. From the outside, I looked like your average, well-established, successful professional. I had my own house in beautiful Vermont, which satisfied my desire to be close to nature, a good job and income, friends for various social engagements, nice neighbors, etc., but I felt a longing for something more. As I continued to devote more time to spiritual pursuits, my work and life circumstances began to feel increasingly uncomfortable. They eventually grew uncomfortable enough that I felt like I had no choice *but* to trust. In other words, I could stay in the familiar discomfort or listen to my inner voice urging me to, in my perception at the time, risk it all. This was a big step for me—the left-brained, analytical, process-everything-to-death person—to take a chance and leave what was superficially comfortable so I could satisfy internal yearnings. Ultimately, I decided to quit my job, sell my house, and move to another state to be with my partner and take steps to pursue my passion.

When life becomes increasingly difficult and frustrating, we begin to see that trust is always the best option. I had escaped the dramatic two-by-four to the head as a lesson, but if I had trusted the earlier whispers, I could have saved myself much frustration and could have started my desired path earlier. So, if *I* can learn to trust, believe me, you can too.

Questions:

1. Describe how, when, or where in your life you have felt, seen, or experienced these concepts.

2. How did you feel as you read the chapter? Did it support or challenge your previous understanding of the material? Explain any changes in how you now view trust and discernment.

3. What stood out to you?

4. Do you trust yourself to make decisions that are for your highest and best? What gets in the way? Explain.

5. Describe a time in the past when you trusted the soft voice of your intuition over the voice of your ego. How did it *feel*? What helped you discern the better choice to make?

6. Choose something in your life now that you would like to change. What is it and why do you desire it to change?

7. Take a few minutes and meditate with the intent to change it. Which voice is speaking to you, the Spirit within or the ego or both? What are they saying about what you would like to change? What are you feeling?

8. Ask for help in discerning the Spirit within over the voice of the ego. Now mediate again on what you would like to change. How do you feel? Describe any changes in the feeling of trusting your intuition.

9. How might you apply any of this material in your life?

~ Chapter 21 ~

Attachment, Addiction & Detachment

He who would be serene and pure needs but one thing, detachment.
— Meister Eckhart

It is difficult to free fools from the chains they revere.
— Voltaire

Detachment is a common concept in many religions and is important for spiritual growth as well. Often, detachment is viewed as a removal of our longing for, gathering of, or assigned importance to worldly things. Given that we are currently living in the three-dimensional plane and require at least some worldly items to sustain our physical form, we want to be able to exist and move through life while using and enjoying necessary or desirable items, but without becoming attached to them.

Attachment & Addiction

The idea of detachment could best be described through its opposite, attachment, which is one of the ego's favorite tools to get us to give away our inner power. The feeling of attachment indicates a holding onto something with an unwillingness to let it go. This can be related to physical objects (like a car, computer, or painting), ideals (like a clean environment or world peace), projects (like a home or work project), thoughts or emotions (like anger at or love for someone), places (like our hometown, home country, or favorite spiritual place), or outcomes (like expecting certain results). Being attached to any of these things essentially bestows them with an aspect of our power, a power we choose to give away to the object, ideal, thought, emotion, place, or outcome. Consequently, they have power *over* us because we fear their loss, consciously or subconsciously. By being attached to them, we also reinforce their place as being *outside* of ourselves.

Addiction is the enhanced energy of attachment through compulsive mental and emotional grasping. In this context, it goes beyond the stereotypical drug, alcohol, or gambling addiction. When we look at our own behaviors, we can all probably find some mental or emotional habit strong enough to create the energy of addiction, whether it is to excitement, victimhood, or some form of action or drama. Any addictive behavior, whether it is to drugs, alcohol, sex, money, exercise, television, the Internet, texting, emotions, multitasking, etc., steals our valuable time and energy. It keeps us desperately scrambling for our *perceived* needs so we remain blocked to seeing the negative aspects of ourselves we don't want to face, the unmet needs beneath the surface. These obsessive habits rob us of our

Attachment, Addiction & Detachment

power, as the ego uses them to take control over our lower mental and emotional bodies. Conscious or subconscious, addictions infuse our aura with the gripping energy of that which is sought, creating an intense artificial need that dominates our time and energy to the detriment of who we truly are. On a deeper level, it denies our divine state.

If we have an addiction and want to continue on the spiritual path, we will benefit greatly from professional help. Constant distraction by forceful physical, mental, or emotional drives makes spiritual learning a challenge because our growth becomes subservient to the addictive urges. As we open to lessons from our addictions and work through the existing binds they have created, we diminish their hold on us and grow to recognize and accept our Truth. (See *Transforming Baggage*)

Note that spiritual seeking can be an attachment or addiction as well. If we constantly feel the pressing need to read more spiritual books, go to more workshops, or learn new spiritual tools and techniques without taking the time to digest and integrate that which we have already learned, then we may be attached to the *process* of learning about spirituality without actually putting it into *practice*. Being preoccupied with constantly learning new things doesn't afford the time or energy to bring the lessons into being.

Many years ago, I had a tai chi instructor who was a little annoyed that some of his American students were learning a number of different tai chi forms before perfecting a basic sequence. He felt that they (or rather, their personalities) put a higher value on knowing the simple mechanics of multiple forms than on doing any single one expertly. What was the point of knowing various forms if they were all performed improperly? What is the use of learning so many new and different spiritual tools if we don't bring them into our daily lives and *live* them?

Detachment

Detachment, on the other hand, reinstates our natural creative power. By relinquishing attached items and outcomes without feeling remorse, anger, guilt, or any other emotion that arises through our separation from them, we accept that whatever the attachments, they may have come to us for a reason, but that reason has now passed. In detachment there is a tacit acknowledgement that the object, ideal, thought, emotion, place, or result no longer has any power over us and that all our internal divine power within cannot be fractured and dissipated by anything external.

That is not to say we can't enjoy objects or places, work on projects, and strive toward ideals. Joy and pleasure are our natural states that we can experience now though activities in this three-dimensional world. However, we can enjoy the experience *without being attached to the results*. An example of this is participating in a sport we love to play just for the experience and not for the outcome of winning. We may intend on winning, but letting go of the end result allows us to relax into the moment, be present, and thus likely play better. The point is that playing in the Now engages us *wholly* in the experience, in life, regardless of what we are doing.

Detachment reduces the amount of energy we spend on things outside ourselves and helps lessen the hold of negative mental and emotional habits. With clearer, purer thoughts, we retain our creative power and a more open channel to divine mind in the present moment, allowing us to flow with life in a joyful and trusting manner. We come to learn that whatever we experience is for our highest good, no matter what. In choosing to see clearly and to learn from the lessons we bring to ourselves, we strengthen the link to divine mind, which provides greater power and clarity to our intentions and manifestations. Thus, we can create our reality, unobstructed by distractions, in alignment with Truth.

Questions:

1. Describe how, when, or where in your life you have felt, seen, or experienced these concepts.

2. How did you feel as you read the chapter? Did it support or challenge your previous understanding of the material? Explain any changes in how you now view attachment, addiction, and detachment.

3. What stood out to you?

4. Choose a current object, ideal, project, thought, emotion, place, or outcome that you feel particularly attached to. Is it an attachment or a habit? Why is it

so important? What does it provide and what needs does it fulfill? Is it necessary to your life?

5. Close your eyes and take a deep breath. Know you are safe. Know you are a perfect creator. Trust in your manifesting abilities. Feel the presence of God within. Take another deep breath.

    Now, reflect on the attachment or habit again. Does it still feel necessary? Can you see it from a broader context? Describe what you are feeling.

6. How might you apply any of this material in your life?

~ Chapter 22 ~

Judgment

How little do they see what really is, who frame their hasty judgment upon that which seems.

– Daniel Webster

We are schooled about judgment from a young age by being taught that our three-dimensional environment is dependent on it. We first learn to identify the world through labels and then in terms of good and bad as we assimilate rules, social norms, expectations, etc. We are trained to judge people, places, and things in order to distinguish what to seek out and what to avoid so we can keep our ego and personality "safe." We continue do this on a regular basis as we identify and categorize people's behaviors, appearances, comments, etc., and we believe these judgments are wise choices because they appeared to have worked well in our early childhood. However, as adult spiritual seekers, we now need to unlearn our reflexive judging so we can see the world neither as good nor bad but rather as a grand schoolyard of lessons for all.

Fundamentally, judging others is a judgment against ourselves, as our world of friends, family, colleagues, and acquaintances provide the mirrors that reflect what we find unacceptable about ourselves. Discomfort arises as something in the other person or situation prods a memory, which calls forth a fearful emotional state, often subconscious, and we rationalize that fear into a judgment about the person, situation, or ourselves. It is one of the ego's tools to foster separation through comparison. Even judging someone in a positive way as opposed to in a negative way produces the same energy of comparison and separation, and it moves us away from oneness.

For example, to say that one person is better looking than another is to give one a higher status of physical beauty, thereby holding them in higher esteem than the other, who is energetically dismissed. The ego has thus created or reinforced a hierarchy, which it loves to do, so that everyone else can be compared to the chosen one. Even if our intentions are positive, we then subconsciously judge ourselves against them, fostering insecurities if we don't measure up. A simple judgment turns into categorizing ourselves against others, encouraging separation, which then plagues us until it is addressed.

Since our judgments of others reflect traits in ourselves, we need to be able to step back and observe how they apply to *us*. We may hate liars because we say we never lie, so why do we hate them? Perhaps we lie to ourselves, saying that we want to do things we really, consciously or subconsciously, don't want to do. The anger at ourselves from the internal dishonesty gets

Judgment

projected outward and we place it as a judgment upon others.

When we find ourselves in judgment, asking *why* we are reacting in that way and trying to witness the judgment as an outside observer helps us begin to understand what that person is mirroring to us. The reason is frequently because we are uncomfortable with that particular aspect of ourselves, and our ego is reacting with denial. This produces a subconscious conflict between our belief system, with all its judgments, and who we are as all-connected, divine beings. It also often points to unresolved stressors such as the discrepancy between the face we present to the world and what we fear others might learn about us if they got to know us better. To move forward spiritually, conflicts such as these need to be reconciled and any guilt or fear addressed.

First, we need to be honest with ourselves, honest about our fears, feelings, judgments, emotions, mental states, etc. Seeing ourselves with clarity brings the opportunity to *accept* who we are, with all our faults, at any given moment. We are the sum total of many energies and acknowledging the existence of judgments and accepting them as a part of ourselves that is not yet healed can be instrumental in helping release them.

When we are consciously aware of these heavier energetic aspects of ourselves and on an ongoing basis begin to notice when they arise, we can minimize their negative effects by stopping their momentum immediately. The longer we consciously or subconsciously *practice* these negative states, the more difficult they are to transform. (See *Reframing*) Anytime we devote energy to something, positive or negative, we sustain that energy. *Any* focus, even worry or intentional avoidance of something we wish to keep away, nourishes that energy on some level. When we can focus on something other than the negative attribute we wish to release, that negative characteristic begins to wither and die because we no longer feed it with energy.

Shining a light on all these negative mental and emotional pieces of ourselves, and *consciously* seeing and knowing them, sets the stage for being able to *choose* whether or not we want to chase, wallow in, or transform them. The choice for transformation is the choice for forgiveness. As we are able to forgive others for their perceived negative attributes, we can begin to apply the forgiveness to ourselves. (See *Fear & Forgiveness*)

Note that our judgments can masquerade as personal preferences when we are attached to them. For example, someone may prefer that their partner not wear makeup because they see it as hiding who they truly are. This is a judgment, not a preference. The person wearing makeup may have other reasons for doing so that have nothing to do with hiding.

Observing and catching ourselves in judgment stops the energy of separation and allows us to choose another response, which helps us move forward in our life with more unity with the world around us.

Judgment

Questions:

1. Describe how, when, or where in your life you have felt, seen, or experienced this concept.

2. How did you feel as you read the chapter? Did it support or challenge your previous understanding of the material? Explain any changes in how you now view judgment.

3. What stood out to you?

4. Identify a judgment you hold about others. It can be anything—weight, beauty, race, culture, attitude, behavior, etc. Describe how you react when confronted by it, including any thoughts, emotions, spoken words, and actions.

5. Why do you think you react in the way you do when judging the above? Is there an aspect of yourself related to that judgment with which you are uncomfortable? Did you grow up in a household that held that judgment? Explore and note your thoughts.

6. Now, look at your process of judging like you were an outside observer watching it unfold. What do you witness? What are you *feeling* as you observe the scene. Do you judge *yourself* judging?

7. Honestly gauge your ability to detach from the judgment. Is the judgment necessary? How has it helped you in your life? How could *not* judging it help you in your life? Explain.

8. How might you apply any of this material in your life?

~ Chapter 23 ~

Fear & Forgiveness

He who cannot forgive breaks the bridge over which he himself must pass.

– George Herbert

Forgiveness is the fragrance that the violet sheds on the heel that has crushed it.

– Mark Twain

Fear is not just a reaction to perceived physical danger or horror movies. It is *the* underlying emotion behind anger, anxiety, sadness, jealousy, judgment, and other such negative emotions, all of which are energetic blocks to our awareness and ongoing awakening. Whether conscious or subconscious, fears are like energetic tumors in our aura, exerting an influence on what energies we invite to us. As we move along our path, the fears we hold bring forth the people and circumstances that resonate to that energy, thus generating the lessons we walk through. These lessons, whether easy or difficult, are *always* beneficial, as they illuminate what we need to transcend in order to find, or rather remember, peace. Lessons do not stop until our fears are dissolved, and our fears cannot be dissolved until we *choose* to overcome them. Considering that our fears are based on false perceptions, to heal ourselves, we must desire to see them from a higher context with the eyes of Truth.

Forgiveness is one way to do this. Forgiveness moves us past this underlying flawed perception that created the fears, allowing us to move forward spiritually with more lightness and clarity.

When we can *observe* our fears, we step above them and see them from the outside as a witness, thereby minimizing their grasp and reducing their power over us. Choosing forgiveness over remaining in fear *immediately* shifts our energy, dissolving the fear and correcting our perception so that we see from the context of our Higher Self. We begin to feel and know the oneness with others because by choosing forgiveness, we acknowledge the divinity in others and ourselves and connect with them through that shared sacredness.

Forgiveness cannot be forced; it must be chosen and allowed to unfold. It is often an ongoing process, as long-standing and intense hurts may need to be forgiven over time by addressing each layer of reinforced pain as each presents itself. By staying focused with the intent to overcome our fears, by realizing that our fears are just tools of the ego to keep us bound to misperceptions and illusions, and by asking for help from our angels and guides, we can find the inner strength to choose forgiveness over wallowing endlessly in the prison of our fears and victimhood. Continually being present to the opportunities for forgiveness allows us to move past the blocks that keep us in limitation. While our ego may try to convince us otherwise, forgiveness reclaims our power instead of relinquishing it.

Ultimately, forgiving others leads to forgiving ourselves. Since the personalities and experiences that present themselves to us are reflections of our inner conscious and subconscious energies, forgiving others is the vehicle that helps bring about self-forgiveness. As we absolve others, we liberate them *and* an aspect of ourselves, eventually resulting in facing only ourselves in the mirror: judgment day, and we are the judge. To forgive ourselves is to love ourselves, and loving ourselves leads to loving all life.

As a personal example, I used to be accustomed to beating myself up about pretty much everything I did during the day. As I would try to fall asleep, I would have the day's scenes replaying through my head. What could I have said in one situation for a better outcome? Why didn't I take the stairs to avoid the crowded elevator with a person with the overpowering perfume? What could I have done to minimize my supervisor's intrusion into my work? Why did I eat that food for lunch that gave me a headache? What could I have done better, in every situation!? Nothing escaped my analysis and it cost me many sleepless nights.

It was not until I started meditating that these questions began to dissipate. I was not yet aware of the concept that my external circumstances reflected my internal world, but I noticed that when I looked at one of these situations from a more loving, meditative space instead of a space of anxiety, the fearful energy lost its power. I didn't realize it then, but in the process of accepting my actions as not "wrong" and in releasing others from fault, I was indirectly forgiving myself for second guessing the activities of the day. Over time, this broke the cycle of spiraling anxiety and fostered the trust in myself that had been previously missing.

Become attuned to noticing when fears arise and forgive both yourself and the other person for your roles. You both created the situation and contracted to learn from it . . . together. Realizing the good of the lesson and creating peace where there once was fear is one of the most powerful ways of uncovering the divine within.

Questions:

1. Describe how, when, or where in your life you have felt, seen, or experienced these concepts.

2. How did you feel as you read the chapter? Did it support or challenge your previous understanding of the material? Explain any changes in how you now view fear and forgiveness.

3. What stood out to you?

4. Describe a situation that puts you in a state of fear.

5. Look at that fear as if you were observing it for the first time *in someone else*. What do you see? What do you feel? What would you say to them about the fear?

6. Realizing that this fear is just a tool of the ego to keep you bound to misperceptions and illusions, ask your

angels to help you see it in Truth. Describe what you think and feel.

7. Why do you think you have this fear? Have there been times when you feel like you've invited circumstances that cause this fear to be present? What might be the lesson it brings? Explain.

8. Being present to the lesson you are uncovering about yourself, if another person is involved, ask for *their* forgiveness for *your* role in the situation. Was that easy or difficult? Does it feel like a mental process or more of an emotional/feeling process? How does that *feel* to you? Explain.

9. Now forgive *them* for the role *they* are playing to bring this fear to *you?* Note your thoughts and emotions.

10. Can you now forgive *yourself* for the role *you* are playing to learn the lesson? Describe what you feel.

11. How might you apply any of this material in your life?

Chapter 24

Dreams

Dreams are the touchstones of our character.
— Henry David Thoreau

The dream state offers wonderful opportunities to observe the metaphors of our attitudes and beliefs. It is a state wherein we lose our analytical thinking so there is no mental processing of the thoughts, images, and emotions that arise, but rather immediate effects of our raw, unrefined reactions to them.

When dreaming, we are in the astral plane where whatever we think happens instantly. If picturing a certain place, we are there. If thinking of a particular object, we have it. It is where we can observe our natural impulses without the direct cause-and-effect, analytical reasoning of our concrete mind.

Our dreams are richly imbued with symbolism, which can show us our true beliefs. We may *think* we know our beliefs consciously, but our dreams can tell us otherwise through symbolic representation of those beliefs without the mental processing that allows us to rationalize or defend our ego-based positions. What we see and feel is pure *us*, with the concrete mind out of the way. Furthermore, our reactions *during* the dream to what we experience can reveal emotional blocks. If we are fearful when we see a snake in a dream, then that may be something to look at more closely once awake. *Why* are we fearful? What can the symbol reveal to us?

The symbolism in dreams can help uncover the blocks to our spiritual growth. For example, if we keep having dreams about conflict but perceive that we have no controversy in our life, it may be an indication that we need to look at our *perception* regarding conflict. We may have an internal struggle that presents itself through anger, anxiety, and frustration instead of obvious, in-your-face fights or disagreements.

Many years ago, I had a dream of being on a group expedition to find a Tarzan-like man in the jungle who had not seen civilization for thirty years and who actively shunned people. When we came upon where he lived, the scene immediately transformed, and I was alone and standing in front of the house in which I grew up. I felt an intense, prickly fear crawl across my skin because it felt like the uncivilized, frightened man was inside the house. I knew I had to enter to face him, so I mustered my courage and entered. Systematically starting with the basement, I moved through every room in the house, never seeing the man but feeling profound dread and anxiety as he seemed to be around every corner ready to jump out and attack. I woke up in a state of paralyzing fear.

As I thought about the dream later that day, I recognized that the uncivilized man was a part of me. He was an element from adolescence, a time dominated by apprehension and angst. The grown-up, fearful man knew only the circumstances of his separation at that age and at that time. Imagine spending thirty years alone and fearful, becoming an adult with only that context from which to view the world. He was just a small part of me, but I knew he had infused who I was as a whole.

Symbolically, the expedition represented my search for Truth, which ultimately was a search for myself. My childhood home represented an old, core consciousness with the basement being the subconscious. The frightened man represented the apprehensions of my adolescence, the fear of fitting into society.

Later in meditation, I consciously returned to the house and re-experienced the fear, this time forgiving the energy of the man, which was really just forgiving myself for not recognizing and nurturing him through the stresses of those times. With that, the heavy energy of the dream, held in my aura and subconscious, released and I felt like an old burden had been taken off my shoulders.

As we grow mentally, emotionally, and spiritually, the qualities and themes of our dreams may change. This is a positive shift, as the "pure us" in the dreams will reflect the transformation to higher energies and corrected belief systems. For example, we may outgrow conflict dreams having resolved some old, long-standing issue from childhood or a past life.

It is possible for someone with intent to enter our dreams. We can protect ourselves from this by affirming before going to sleep that we are protected and by asking that only that which is for our highest good come to us.

We can also communicate with others when *they* are dreaming or daydreaming. For example, when we intend on forgiving others for their involvement in a difficult situation, they can more easily accept that forgiveness when in the dream state, as their personality defenses are lowered. In addition, friends and family who have passed away may find it is easiest to communicate with us when we are dreaming, letting us know they are still with us in spirit. So, seeing our grandmother in a dream may actually be a visit from her and not a metaphor or symbol of something else.

To gain the most benefit from your dreams, write them down as soon as you awaken. Within minutes of waking, substantial details often fade. Note any characters, situations, or symbols and your feelings toward them. They are *yours*, first and foremost. You may experience certain characters and symbols because they mean a particular thing to you and you alone. Having a good dream interpretation book can help define some themes and details, but fundamentally it is *your* story, and you were shown what *you* needed to see. Only you can fully interpret it.

The symbolism of the characters in our dreams (which most of the time represent an aspect of ourselves), the objects, settings, situations, etc. tell a story. Put your dream story back together with the symbolic knowledge from your research and personal perspective.

Meditate on the theme. You will be surprised at what you learn about yourself.

Some examples of dream symbolism:

- The characteristics, attitudes, and behaviors of people generally represent aspects of ourselves. Even animals or objects can hold attributes of the dreamer. Is that person in the dream judging you? Then you may be harboring judgments about others and ultimately yourself.
- Vehicles generally represent our manner of moving forward. Did your car break down? You may feel unable to or lack the desire to continue with something you are working on.
- Being chased generally represents feeling threatened. What/who are you running from?
- Water generally represents emotions. Is the sea dark and choppy or clear and calm?
- Death generally represents the end of something, making room for something new. It is an energy that often indicates transformation. Did your neighbor's cat die in the dream? What does that represent to you?

Questions:

1. Describe how, when, or where in your life you have felt, seen, or experienced this concept.

2. How did you feel as you read the chapter? Did it support or challenge your previous understanding of the material? Explain any changes in how you now view dreams.

3. What stood out to you?

4. Describe a dream where you remember the details. If you've had a recurring dream that you remember, use that one.

5. What actions and details seem important in the dream? These are your primary symbols. Make three columns in your journal, the first labeled Action-Detail-Symbol, the second labeled My Meaning, and the third labeled Other Meaning. Write down the actions, prominent details, and symbols from the dream in the first column. Without looking up the symbolism, reflect on what *you* think the meaning of each is and write it in the My Meaning column.

6. Now that you've recognized some symbolism, describe the dream again. Has the meaning of the story changed?

7. What do you think is the lesson(s) of the dream?

8. If you desire, look up your symbols in a dream interpretation book or online. (Note that there may be many different interpretations of a given symbol.) Write the symbolism in the Other Meaning column.

9. Does this add clarity to the symbolism of your dream? How does it change the meaning, story, or how you view the lesson(s)?

10. How might you apply any of this material in your life?

~ Chapter 25 ~

Distractions

Obstacles are those frightful things you see when you take your eyes off your goal.

– Henry Ford

We often look forward in time, taking ourselves out of the present moment, and expect that something we think will be bad will be *really* bad and something we think will be good will be *really* good. Our ego distracts us from the present moment by creating this kind of anticipatory excitement to keep us too disoriented to purely *be* in the Now. Similarly, ego often resurrects past events by dipping into soul memory to produce the same effect. Either way, being distracted by thoughts or emotions forward or backwards in time disrupts our ability to truly experience life in the moment. Because we radiate the dramatic energy of expectation or an anxious or fearful energy of a past experience, we draw to ourselves circumstances that reflect exactly those energies. Our ego wants us to *perceive* excitement rather than allow us to *live* and *feel* the joy, love, and peace of the present. We can view life as a great drama where we need ego's protection, as the ego wants us to believe, or we can see it as a collection of endless present moments, constantly guiding us back to remembering our Spirit within.

Modern culture has trained us to increasingly *react* to stimuli as opposed to *respond* to stimuli. With our fast-paced, technologically-driven culture of instant gratification and quick fixes, we seem to be always on the lookout for the ping of a text or e-mail, or jingle of a cell phone call. Studies show that for many, the reactions to these pings and rings approach addictive behavior. (See *Attachment, Addiction & Detachment*)

We accept operating in this way because we seem to demand it of each other, craving rapid responses to our messages and worrying when someone doesn't respond immediately or within a few minutes. This establishes the energy of living not for ourselves but for others, and our lives become the dim reflection of what *they* are saying and doing. When we are repeatedly in the mode of having our radar out to what *others* are doing, we are not *with ourselves*. Energetically, this diminishes who we are *to* ourselves by giving our power to those around us. The back and forth with each other (like with frenetic texting and social media engagement) provides a continuous feedback loop that wastes our energy and takes us further and further from who we truly are. How can we know ourselves when we are standing in a hall of mirrors reflecting all of our social media "friends"?

Reacting to something carries an energy of anxiety and jumpiness, of being at the beck and call of someone, something, or a situation that is not our own. We may feel compelled to react immediately, which may come from some old, buried, psycho-emotional block of needing attention, which we didn't receive as a child if we didn't instantly respond. Whatever the reason, *who are we* if we spend our days reacting to other people's thoughts, especially if many of them are unproductive and barren of meaning to us?

So, if we find ourselves being pulled in many directions, multitasking, or experiencing life overly influenced by the others' energies, we need to begin to notice our reactions and instead choose to respond consciously. We need to begin to see that what happens around us does not need to be stressful because everything is a learning opportunity that we energetically asked for in one form or another. When we can understand that and truly *know* it, we can relax into the moment and allow our Spirit within to shine, accepting all situations as wonderful learning opportunities.

Distractions have been one of my greatest struggles on the spiritual path, so I am certainly speaking to myself here as well as to you, the reader. Even while writing this book, I struggled with many distractions, including some that I willingly engaged and encouraged. For example, having the Internet constantly available was sometimes an issue for me. Whenever I ran into some writer's block or was wrestling with editing a difficult passage, I used it as an excuse to check email again or check news updates to avoid muscling through the work. It didn't matter that I had already checked email five times in the past twenty minutes! I was energetically "checking out" of the present moment because I had met some resistance while writing.

We do this all the time. When we dislike a task or find it difficult, we find things to distract us. My most highly focused writing time was when I went to a quiet office that had no Internet. There, without my most familiar diversion, I could really focus and work through both the easy and more difficult tasks.

Even if we believe we have a personality that keeps us from focusing, there is *always* something we can do to minimize distractions, like finding a place without an Internet connection. It is a matter of will and action. When we strongly *believe* we can focus, we manifest an environment more conducive to doing what we desire to do. Trust me, what would have distracted us will still be there when we are done. My email didn't go away and I didn't miss any news by going online hours later. Finding the inner strength to ignore and overcome our distracting habits will dissipate their power and allow us to more fully realize what the present moment brings.

Questions:

1. Describe how, when, or where in your life you have felt, seen, or experienced this concept.

2. How did you feel as you read the chapter? Did it support or challenge your previous understanding of the material? Explain any changes in how you now view distractions.

3. What stood out to you?

Distractions

4. Do you frequently look forward in time in anticipation of what is to come, investing energy into thinking about what an upcoming experience is going to be like? How deeply do you get mentally and emotionally into projecting situations?

5. Does the emotional excitement/drama you anticipate always happen? How does the actual event compare to what you have imagined?

6. Do you often think about past experiences, allowing them to spin endlessly in your head? How much do they affect your emotions?

7. How reactive are you to texts, e-mails, and phone calls? Do you feel guilty or irresponsible if you don't answer or respond immediately? What do you feel when you hear the ping of a text or e-mail on your phone? Are you anxious if you are away from your phone for a length of time?

8. Take a moment to sit comfortably with your eyes closed. Take a few deep breaths. Feel the energy of your aura fill with light as you breathe in. Breathe out any tension, thoughts, and emotions—anything that is not of the light.

    Keep breathing slowly and deeply. Feel the vitality of your physical body and aura as the energy lightens. Be present with it. *Experience* the moment as a being of energy. There is no past or future. Everything is in the Now. Stay with this feeling for as long as you are comfortable.

How did you feel? More present? Anxious? Scattered? Could you let go of remembering and anticipating and be in the present moment? Describe your experience.

9. How might you apply any of this material in your life?

~ Chapter 26 ~

Care of the Physical

To keep the body in good health is a duty . . . otherwise we shall not be able to keep our mind strong and clear.

– Buddha

Every level of our consciousness and energy influences the physical form. Our body is a manifested amalgamation of our thoughts, emotions, beliefs, planned contracts, perceived karmic debts, soul memories, and influences from our Higher Self. It reflects the effects of the choices we made to come into this incarnation for learning the lessons we feel are necessary for our growth. Our particular body type, race, ethnicity, and disabilities are examples of these effects.

Our body *is* our "temple" in that the care we take of it indicates how we view ourselves consciously and, even more importantly, subconsciously. Are we emotionally stressed, causing muscular tension? Do we smoke, showing a lack of respect for our form? Do we sit hunched over a computer or slouched on a couch in front of the television all day, closing off our heart center? Consciously choosing to take care of our physical body aligns our intent with the natural perfection within, which ripples through the layers of our aura and our mental and emotional bodies, raising our energy on all levels.

Being spiritual is not about denying or forsaking the body; it is about respecting it as a vehicle. There are many practices that profess to help us physically so we can grow spiritually, such as yoga, vegetarianism, and chi gong to name a few. Indeed, some practices may result in better physical and mental health by reducing stress, lowering blood pressure, helping us concentrate or lose weight, or generally making us feel good. And when we feel healthy, we have more confidence and are better able to focus and raise our consciousness up beyond the earth plane.

Proper exercise and diet, of course, are important parts of being a healthy human being. With the advent of the Internet and easy access to news and entertainment twenty-four hours a day, many people sit and have their faces buried in screens all day. This is not healthy on a number of levels: studies have shown that children who play outside more have less of a need for glasses; people who exercise are physically, mentally, and sexually healthier; those who sit less live longer; and people who eat less fast food have lower incidents of heart disease. Note, however, that although these studies may be accurate, any one individual's results are still dependent on their belief system and life contracts. For example, someone who sits all day may live to be one hundred ten years old and someone who is always moving and exercising may live to be only forty-five.

Care of the Physical

Another self-care practice is maintaining good posture. A relaxed yet upright bearing can help bring us into energetic alignment because standing up straight opens the solar plexus and heart connections to our energy bodies, important connections for spiritual growth. A slouching posture limits these connections. There is a field of study called bioenergetics that explores body psychology, looking at physical structure and tension and correlating emotional issues to these physical blocks. Some basic exploration in this area can help reveal long-standing, psycho-emotional sources of dis-ease.

Even though our causal thoughts affect our physical form, our body still needs to be taken care of appropriately when we find ourselves in a state of dis-ease. As much as we want to correct the *source* of any physical ailment (i.e. the non-physical cause), there are times we must work with our dis-ease in the three-dimensional plane to keep our bodily vehicle healthy. Until we are fully aligned with our Spirit within to naturally be in perfect health, physical ailments may require healing from other avenues. And as mentioned previously, it can be difficult to live from a spiritual context when the body is in pain. (See *Healing*)

We need to use discernment in choosing physical remedies. If having back pain, selecting spinal surgery *before* trying other less invasive methods may not be the best first option, as surgery cuts our etheric body as well as our physical body, which increases the time it takes to heal. Simpler methods may be more appropriate. Our society often promotes the quick fix without addressing the true underlying cause, which is really our thinking and emotions stemming from our belief system.

Even strictly on the physical level, symptoms can obscure the somatic origin *through* which our mis-thoughts (thoughts not aligned with our Spirit within) create the dis-ease. Non-obvious physical conduits of illness such as diet, hormonal, or other imbalances can sometimes be elusive to an accurate diagnosis. Allopathic doctors can only do what they have been trained to do in the limited time they have, which often keeps them from seeing patients as holistic beings. This can sometimes result in treating *symptoms* in the physical body more than the *cause* of the symptoms, and it doesn't even come close to addressing the underlying belief system, which is the true cause.

Use sound judgment when choosing how to physically address an illness or injury. Don't have brain surgery for a hangover and don't take a pill simply to numb yourself to your surroundings. (Note that this is not medical advice but rather common sense.) Physicians and other healers or modalities should be used with discernment. (See *Trust & Discernment*)

So, if someone has a heart problem, what is the true cause? Even though heart surgery may be recommended to correct the issue, ultimately the individual must be ready to give up the dis-ease on all levels for long-term healing. The primary *physical* cause may be that the person is a smoker, eats fast food every day, is a loner with no social support system, and often sits at home slouched on the couch. All these things can contribute to physically weakening the heart to the point of dis-ease where it eventually needs drastic intervention like surgery to work correctly.

However, on a *non-physical* level, the person may have chosen to experience (in other words, contracted) the heart problem, which can come from an old, established belief of not being worthy of love. A severe heart issue can be the triggering event that enhances their life because it makes them realize that they need to not only accept care from others, but also treat their body, and themselves, better. Through exercise, a better diet, and quitting smoking, they should begin to feel healthier physically and mentally, which creates a confidence that was previously missing. (Note that sometimes a physical intervention is necessary to take care of an acute problem first.) With that confidence, they stand up straighter, which opens the heart chakra, allowing a better connection with their higher energies. Subsequently, everything in their life starts to improve as the Spirit within expresses more clearly through them, inviting in higher energies, including love, as they allow others to help them heal. Their mind *chooses* to be healthy, which leads to healing the physical heart *and* they successfully learn the lesson they came into this incarnation to learn. When we walk through a physical manifestation of our struggles, it is a sign to look for the lesson it holds.

Our physical form and the interactions we experience on the earth plane are our best opportunity for spiritual growth. We can learn and grow between incarnations, but our growth has more traction when done in this three-dimensional plane. It is like watching someone drive a car in a movie versus actually driving it ourselves. Seeing it in a movie doesn't give us the full experience.

The physical form is a reflection of how we *think* and *feel* about ourselves. When it is healthy, we do not swirl down a path of physical distractions and annoyances and so are better able to manage the spiritual growth we desire. Furthermore, having a positive attitude toward our body infuses us with confidence, which keeps our energies higher and allows tension in all its forms to slide past instead of stick. How we feel about ourselves becomes how we *are*, on many levels. Why not stay positive and healthy and experience life through a perfect, fully-functioning physical body? It is certainly more enjoyable than the alternative.

Questions:

1. Describe how, when, or where in your life you have felt, seen, or experienced this concept.

2. How did you feel as you read the chapter? Did it support or challenge your previous understanding of the material? Explain any changes in how you now view caring for your physical form.

3. What stood out to you?

4. How do you currently take care of your physical body?

Care of the Physical

5. Describe any physical issues you experience on a recurring basis. If none are recurring, then choose a few recent issues.

6. What do you think these issues represent?

7. Do you feel that any of these issues inhibit or limit your spiritual growth? Explain.

8. What changes can you make to better take care of your physical form?

9. How might you apply any of this material in your life?

~ Chapter 27 ~

Disconnecting to Connect

Climb the mountains and get their good tidings. Nature's peace will flow into you as sunshine flows into trees. The winds will blow their own freshness into you, and the storms their energy, while cares will drop away from you like the leaves of autumn.

– John Muir

Sometimes we need to get away from our regular lives to refresh our perspective on life. We get caught up in the routines of daily living and working and begin to lose perspective on everything else. Sure, we think we have perspective because we get our news from the Internet or television, or we e-mail with Aunt Mildred about the family, and we think we're connected. But connected to what?

Do we not choose the news we wish to view? Do we not tune out Aunt Mildred when she drones on about something we have no interest in and doesn't affect us? Do we not have the time to focus on anything but what immediately surrounds us? What we are *not* doing is looking at one thing that benefits all other aspects of our life. Obscured by our busyness is something that can help change how we view all situations. Namely, *we don't spend quality time with ourselves.*

When we are running around with lists of things to do, we are outside ourselves. We put a false importance on the external and neglect our internal self. We push people away because we feel the need to get something done, something that seems so vastly important at the time that we make decisions we regret.

Our culture, both work and personal, has become so busy that we don't have time for anything but the screens in front of our faces. The problem is that when we are constantly bombarded by stimuli, we are always in an energy of being reactive to outside circumstances, directly or through the proxy of electronic communications. Who are we then but a reflection of those stimuli? Sure, we may put our own unique personality spin on our reactions, but by being driven by what is outside of us, we become *someone else*. We reflect the collective energies of the world, those energies that we say we are trying to escape from because we are on the spiritual path. Those reflections *become who we are*. It is indeed ironic that we are the creators and sustainers of those energies when we say we desire to rise above them.

We, individually and as a society, are in an endless loop of being reactive, feeding the collective anxiety and fast-paced culture around us, then reacting to it, thereby feeding it, and so on. If we are waiting for the other guy to stop the cycle, we are in for a long ride. It is truly up to us to stop the reacting, end the feeding, break the cycle, and show others something else to respond to like

Disconnecting to Connect

love, joy, positivity, and forgiveness. If those aren't the energies we are radiating, then what are?

So how do we move forward spiritually? We must get over lamenting past actions and get to really know ourselves. The past is the past. We made the best decisions we could at the time based on who we were and the information we had. Now we accept the lessons that came with our choices and choose to make better decisions going forward.

Connecting with ourselves puts the continuous mirroring of energies in perspective. Finding time to be alone, particularly out in nature, gives us a break from those reflections and makes us more in tune with the natural world, including our inner nature. We discover the physical, mental, emotional, and spiritual space to breathe without any judgments. Taking time for ourselves is not a chore but rather a nourishment of the soul and a reinforcement of our connection to God. It is the most important connection we can make during the day.

But we must remember to leave our cell phone at home.

Questions:

1. Describe how, when, or where in your life you have felt, seen, or experienced this concept.

2. How did you feel as you read the chapter? Did it support or challenge your previous understanding of the material? Explain any changes in how you now view disconnecting from your "regular" life.

Everything I Wanted to Know About Spirituality...

3. What stood out to you?

4. Do you make lists of things to do? How much do you value your lists? How would you feel if you didn't make lists?

5. Do you think you reflect others' energies during the day or are you always centered in yourself? Explain, and be honest with yourself.

6. Describe the last time you disconnected from electronic devices and spent time *by* yourself... *with* yourself. How long ago was it? If you can't think of anything, then put down this book, shut off your cell phone, and go take a walk, in nature if possible.

7. How did it feel? Were you able to truly "disconnect"? How much more grounded and centered do you now feel?

8. How might you apply any of this material in your life?

~ Chapter 28 ~

Being Uncomfortable

If you do not change direction, you may end up where you are heading.

— Lao Tzu

Discomfort is nothing more than a sign that we are listening to a voice other than our Higher Self. It is an internal struggle that calls us to recognize that our current ego reactions (anxiety, fear, bodily tension, guilt, obsessive thoughts, etc.) are at odds with our inner divine light. When we feel tension on any level (physically, mentally, or emotionally), it is this conflict manifesting as an opportunity to choose to listen to Spirit instead of the ego. This can be difficult, as ego always shouts over Spirit's quiet promptings.

Imagine if something in our life isn't working and we are growing increasingly frustrated with our situation. This presents the opportunity to consider which voice is drawing our attention. Something needs to change or we stay stuck in our distress. Maybe we are in a job we don't like, are trying to lose a few pounds but are having difficulty, desire to grow spiritually but keep getting sidetracked, or are in a relationship that is fraught with conflict but we consistently avoid "the talk" to work through it. Whatever it is, we have to stop and identify what is building the frustration and set about taking steps to better understand what is needed to see the truth of the circumstances.

Easier said than done, right? Well, if we think we are unhappy now, how do we think it will feel a month or a year down the road when we are further entrenched in the situation?

Uncomfortable states of being are signals that the ego is in control. If we don't address the issues that created and continue to create the discomfort, the ego *stays* in control. We need to look at challenging circumstances from a higher context and focus our intent on transforming them in order to cultivate joy, love, and peace. This means *choosing* to change our circumstances, *asking* for guidance (from physical or non-physical beings—see *Asking for Help*), and *trusting* that what we decide to do is for our highest good. (See *Trust & Discernment*)

Note that sometimes there are action steps to take and sometimes it is about *allowing*. When we set our intent, trust, and allow, the answers always come. We may get indications to take physical steps, think about the issue differently, or relax and wait for a particular set of circumstances, but trusting that what we are prompted to do (or not do) always brings about a course of action (or non-action) that helps us learn the lesson and move in the direction toward which Spirit is ever guiding us.

Consider the constant small drip in the sink that we never get around to fixing. We hear it occasionally and it

Being Uncomfortable

bothers us, but we say we'll take care of it later. We keep ignoring it and it continues to bother us, and we notice that it is becoming louder and more frequent over time, but we continue to procrastinate addressing it. Finally, when it is no longer a drip, drip, drip but a stream of water, we take action. Lo and behold, the fix was less painful and took less time than anticipated, something we could have done when we first noticed the problem. Think of how much aggravation we could have avoided if we had repaired it earlier.

Continuous, small frustrations like the unaddressed drip of a faucet or squeak of a doorknob can be more stress inducing than major events like breaking an arm or leg, which can be shorter and more acute but at least have an ending date. The key is to notice when we begin to feel discomfort, observe what the tension is showing us, and address it immediately instead of letting it grow, fester, and further irritate us. Avoidance only serves to compound our frustration because we become increasingly mad at ourselves for not directly facing the situation.

Ego is always telling us that change is scary because it wants us to see *itself* as our protector. It directs us to believe in the dramatic illusion around us and therefore continues to usurp our power by keeping us frozen in our difficult, painful, or unsatisfying circumstances. Ego makes us feel that it is better to stay with what we know than to take a risk with something new.

Regardless, we find that as Spirit gently urges us forward, the tension of our situation increases while ego attempts to remain in control. This internal struggle becomes progressively more uncomfortable until it *outweighs our fear of change*, so we often *do* wind up taking care of the situation, but only after much added aggravation. We finally recognize that we will remain uncomfortable unless and until we address the inner conflict. Why not nip it in the bud and move on with our life in peace, joy, and love?

Our Higher Self prods us ever forward on our spiritual path through uncomfortable situations, but we must be willing to hear its voice. Noticing that a situation is misaligned with our highest good requires a change in our thought processes, one that causes us to think and move in new and different ways. This aligns us further with our inner light, dissolving the blocks that prevent us from being who we are in Truth. We then can more easily find the path we are meant to tread.

We can think of being uncomfortable as states that indicate path corrections, nudging us toward what we *genuinely* desire to do, and to be. We need not be afraid of who we are and of accepting who we want to become.

Questions:

1. Describe how, when, or where in your life you have felt, seen, or experienced this concept.
2. How did you feel as you read the chapter? Did it support or challenge your previous understanding of the material? Explain any changes in how you now view being uncomfortable.

Being Uncomfortable

3. What stood out to you?

4. Identify something in your life with which you are physically, mentally, or emotionally uncomfortable. Describe what it is, when it started, and how the uncomfortable feeling may have built up over time.

5. What about it makes you feel uncomfortable and why do you think you feel that way because of it? What do you perceive is the lesson being brought to you?

6. Can you take steps today to address the issue? What steps will you take? How will these steps alleviate the uncomfortable feeling?

7. How might you apply any of this material in your life?

~ Chapter 29 ~

Phenomena

Miracles, in the sense of phenomena we cannot explain, surround us on every hand: life itself is the miracle of miracles.
— George Bernard Shaw

All phenomena are empty.
— Bodhidharma

As we explore and grow on the spiritual path, we may be exposed to what many experience as "exciting" phenomena within the fields of psychism, mediumship, energy healing, spiritual healing, or altered states of consciousness. We may encounter phenomena with a practitioner or on our own, but while these disciplines and experiences can provide value, we must be careful not to be seduced or entranced by them.

Anything that seems to bend the rules of three-dimensional time and space often challenges our belief system, but as spiritual seekers, sometimes that is exactly what we are looking for. Experiencing something very different from what we believe is our reality can be exciting, as we may view it as a validation of our spiritual efforts, a signpost of attainment on the path, that grandma really is around us and helping us, etc. These are not bad things. In fact, if we experience them, then we are meant to for some greater understanding.

However, what often happens is that our ego uses the experience to further dig its claws into our mental and emotional bodies. Then we wind up fixating on the phenomena and become attached to the idea that we were a particular so-and-so in a past life, think how cool it is that the angels are speaking directly to us, or think that such-and-such is going to happen because our dead great-grandfather showed up and said so. While these experiences may be exciting, when viewed in the context of healing, they can serve to align us with Truth or distract us from it.

Even if the information we receive in a psychic or mediumistic reading is perfectly accurate, it is important to see the experience for what it is: information, validation, and potential healing. To hold onto the event itself and talk about it with our friends for months or years misses the point of the information or experience. It happened to us and for us so we can learn and grow from it. Staying attached to the encounter and information keeps us where we were energetically at that time and inhibits the flow of subsequent lessons. Accept the gift in it and move on. Trust there is so much more.

Attachment to phenomena can also occur through holding onto the need to continue to experience a particular discipline. For example, we might go to a psychic every few months and are able to move forward and integrate the information each time into our spiritual growth, but we may be stuck on the *need* to go for occasional psychic readings, craving our "psychic fix" periodically. This attachment eventually inhibits our personal growth because we are relying on someone else, something outside of us. Ultimately, we need to choose to go within and trust our own inner guidance, even if it doesn't satisfy the ego's desire for details and confirmation. This is where transformation happens.

So, by all means, go to a psychic or medium, talk with your angels or passed-on relatives, feel the otherworldly experience of an energy healing session, but note that your spiritual growth is always dependent upon *you* and *your* willingness to accept a change in your belief system, not on any practitioner or metaphysical experience. The phenomena are just that, phenomena within a world you are trying to transcend.

Questions:

1. Describe how, when, or where in your life you have felt, seen, or experienced this concept.

2. How did you feel as you read the chapter? Did it support or challenge your previous understanding of the material? Explain any changes in how you now view phenomena.

3. What stood out to you?

4. Have you ever experienced anything that seemed to bend the known scientific rules of space and time? Examples include having a psychic or mediumistic

reading, an energy healing session, and an out-of-body experience. Describe the experience and what about it that qualified it as phenomena to you.

5. How did you feel when you experienced it? Were you excited, scared, peaceful, or sad?

6. Why do you think the emotion you experienced came up? What did you learn? Can you discern the lesson involved?

7. Would you want to have that experience again? Why? How will repeating it help you on your spiritual path?

8. How might you apply any of this material in your life?

~ Chapter 30 ~

Discernment with Teachers

A teacher's purpose is not to create students in his own image, but to develop students who can create their own image.
— Author Unknown

On our quest for oneness, we may be exposed to many, many teachers. Depending on our path and inclinations, we may encounter teachings of spirituality through instructors of yoga, meditation, energy work, healing, psychic or mediumship development, psycho-spiritual counseling, etc. We may also come across various authors and workshop presenters who propose that their method or system is the only process through which we will find what we are looking for and that we must stay with their teachings to gain the full benefit. In addition, we may encounter teachers or practitioners with a collection of letters after their names and a wall full of certifications. They may even teach continuing education in their field, adding an air of professionalism to what they do.

Having been exposed to many different spiritual teachers over the years, I have developed a somewhat skeptical eye. Some of these instructors are legitimate and wonderful educators, but I have seen many claims and promotions of certain certifications and abilities that are disingenuous at best when examined. Scratch the surface, and what do we see? Some examples:

- A company created to "license" individuals as Spiritual Healers. I'm not aware of any U.S. state that licenses anything spiritual. This essentially can be bought on the Internet.
- A Certificate of Completion being promoted as "Certified." Does this mean that someone is a Certified Medium because they took an afternoon workshop once on mediumship?
- Someone with no formal background in counseling or therapy calling themselves a Psycho-spiritual Therapist or Counselor. What if they bring up something from the client's past that they don't know how to process with them because they haven't had any therapeutic training? Aside from ethical issues, it can leave the client in a fragile and unsafe state.
- "Coaches" and coaching programs that go beyond their scope of training and attempt to provide or teach counseling or therapy.
- Someone who can't seem to get their life together preaching how to get *your* life together.

Granted, some practitioners and teachers with multiple certifications and several degrees may be ideal to study with for a time, until it is time *not* to study with them. When we get to a place where we feel drawn to look for another person or system to help us on our journey, heed that inner call. We have learned what we needed, and it is time to move on. We each must find our *own* way, and that may mean studying with certain people for a time, only to find that we outgrow them or get to a place where we need something different.

For me, an indicator of *genuine* intent of teachers has been enthusiasm and humility. Some of these teachers have impressive credentials and some do not, but they share an enthusiasm for the material and an excitement about teaching it, about *living* it. In fact, *being* the teachings *is* the ultimate teaching tool as it models how we can live the lessons.

Practice discernment when deciding with whom you wish to study. (See *Trust & Discernment*) I tend to be more discerning with teachers who have a well-oiled business and marketing machine behind them because it often feels more like a business relationship than a sincere teacher-student relationship. Although the material may hold Truth, it can feel like the presentation of that Truth is being distorted by the business. We may learn, but we also need to understand where the lesson ends and where the business or "cult of personality" of the teacher begins.

Genuine teachers are happy to see us and would be happy to see us again, and they don't press hard for us to attend additional workshops or seminars. They just inform us of them. These teachers trust that they and we are both there to teach and learn and that is the reason we have come together. If it happens again, great. If not, then they accept that other adventures and experiences are needed. No stress. No worries.

Humble, enthusiastic, genuine teachers do not have an interest in our returning to an additional seminar or buying a recent book beyond their desire for us to grow spiritually. Rather, they recognize that everyone is on their own path and that our attendance at one seminar is a wonderful opportunity for growth for both of us and that we will take it with us in whatever direction we desire. There is no expectation, guilt, or any other emotion involved to attempt to entice us further into their particular teachings. It is our choice. To a good spiritual teacher, it is always our choice.

The good spiritual teacher's job is to light *our* way, assisting us on *our* path to bring us to a place where we can match or surpass them in knowledge and wisdom. They desire us to take their teachings to a new level, a new level for *us*. Everyone has a unique path, and there is no shame in going from one teacher or system to another to increase our understanding, as long as we are not doing it to avoid doing the hard work ourselves, on ourselves, because that is where the growth happens.

Even though we may seek "formal" instructors, everyone we meet is a potential teacher if we but open our eyes to what they present. It is the *feeling* we get from someone that indicates if he or she can help illuminate our path. It is also the *feeling* we get from whatever system or method they may be teaching, if any. Trust those feelings. They reside in our solar plexus, quite literally. In other words, trust your gut and your heart.

Questions:

1. Describe how, when, or where in your life you have felt, seen, or experienced this concept.

2. How did you feel as you read the chapter? Did it support or challenge your previous understanding of the material? Explain any changes in how you now view teachers and how to discern amongst them.

3. What stood out to you?

4. Describe a few different teachers you've had on the spiritual path (or non-spiritual teachers). What was their energy like? How did you feel when you were with them? How did you feel when you left their class, workshop, or seminar?

5. Assess these teachers in terms of how genuine they were or are. Describe how you came to each assessment.

6. Choose one teacher from your description above that is not a current teacher. What did you learn from them and why do you not study with them anymore? Do you feel you outgrew them in some way?

7. How might you apply any of this material in your life?

~ Chapter 31 ~

Miscellaneous Thoughts

"The time has come," the Walrus said,
"To talk of many things:
Of shoes--and ships--and sealing-wax--
Of cabbages--and kings--
And why the sea is boiling hot--
And whether pigs have wings."

– Lewis Carroll

Mistakes

There is no failure. We inevitably perceive that we make mistakes, but in truth, mistakes cannot be made. Learning is about making decisions and recognizing the lessons, and all lessons have a gift. When what we choose doesn't result in desired outcomes, we can use those opportunities to view what transpired from a higher context and, in our desire to grow, choose better next time.

Unless all our energy is perfectly aligned with our intent and we can view our actions from the higher perspective of seeing the lessons, we will *feel* failure on some level. This is ego judging our experiences, which will happen multiple times, more times than we can count, until we begin to recognize ego's handiwork. But we will also succeed more times than we can count, and every success moves us forward as a brighter point of light in the world. However, it may not always look like beneficial spiritual growth from the outside. It is in *accepting* the lessons as gifts that provides us our spiritual awakening.

Recognizing that we have chosen unwisely is an indication that we are conscious of our choices and are working toward bettering ourselves. Like with reframing, when we feel we have made a mistake, we need to simply pick ourselves up, learn from our choice and experience, and move forward confidently. When we do this, we are *already* past the perceived failure. It is what we learn from the experience that determines our energy moving forward and how we function next time.

Channeling

Channeling is a process of bringing forth information from a non-earthly source *through* a physical form. (Some limit the definition strictly to "trance" channeling and call other types of channeling mental mediumship.) Channeled messages can be intuitive, as in having a feeling or knowingness of information beyond the physical, or mediumistic, where messages are communicated directly through a medium from discarnate beings.

There are many different levels of channeling, with trance channeling being the rarest. This is when the medium's physical form is *entirely* appropriated by an

Miscellaneous Thoughts

entity in order to bring a message. It can take years and even lifetimes of preparation to become this kind of channel because the human vehicle needs to fully trust and accept that they will be taken care of while the channeled entity is occupying their body.

In our spiritual searching, we may come across books and audios of material channeled from discarnate beings. There is much wisdom in some of these materials, but use discernment. Some may be written or spoken in a language that doesn't resonate with us (at the time) or is on a topic that holds little interest. If this is the case, know that there is other information that will feel more appropriate. Knowledge and the right material will present itself when we are open and ready for it.

Because someone claims to (and actually does) channel information from an angel or guide doesn't mean that that channeled entity speaks in our best interests. There are many lower energetic beings who speak through channels, and even the channels themselves may not be aware of the level on which communications occur. As always, discern if the channel and the information resonate deep within. Just because someone tells us the material brought forth is from an angel or guide doesn't mean that it is or that it is on a level that is good for our growth. Trust your instincts. (See *Trust & Discernment* and *Discernment with Teachers*)

The Christ

The Christ energy is more than the man, Jesus of Nazareth (Yeshua). It is that aspect of us that sees with unconditional love and knows, truly knows, the connection with others through that love. Spiritual growth is the continual opening to the Christ energy so that we are *living* embodiments of it here on the earth plane, as Jesus was.

The Holy Spirit

Although decidedly a Christian term, the concept of the Holy Spirit is important to understand. Whatever name it may be called, the Holy Spirit is that aspect of God that *transforms* our misunderstandings and misperceptions into Truth. It is the action-based aspect of the God within. Although the responsibility is ours to do spiritual work to correct our erroneous thinking that we are separate from others, the Holy Spirit can be called upon to actively transform that flawed thinking.

For this to happen, we must *trust* and let go of all doubts. (See *Trust & Discernment*) Trusting, believing, and allowing the Holy Spirit to do its work, and for us to accept the Truth of the situation, transforms our blocked energy so we again see with eyes of Truth.

Heaven & Hell

Heaven is feeling and being in perfect oneness with God and all things. Hell is *everything* short of that feeling, including anything related to fear, anger, guilt, depression, shame, or any other negative emotion. Those emotions are reflections of the inner conflict in human beings, who are perfect creators. A simple way to state it is that heaven and hell are *our* respective experiences of the Spirit within and the ego.

What we create generates the heaven or hell we walk through. We think or do something that projects that energy out in front of us, and then we step in it, call it heaven or hell, and wonder where it originated. It came from within us. *We* are the creators of our own world, be it joyful or miserable, and only *we* can choose the heaven or hell we want to be in, or more appropriately, which we want to *be*. (See *There Is Only Now*) We must choose more wisely so we can truly transcend the hell of our miscreations and *be* in heaven through seeing with the eyes of Truth.

Religion

Man created religions in an attempt to make sense of and experience the divine. Religions provide a level of structure that is appealing to many people for studying that which is believed to be holy. Some individuals find going within difficult. To better know themselves, they feel they need a support structure imposed from the outside in the form of dogma, ceremonies, rituals, or other such organization.

Many religions contain great spiritual truths within their stories and myths, which are often wrapped in beautifully crafted metaphors and allegories. Since spirituality is the *experience* of the divine within and religion is mankind's attempt to understand and communicate that connection with God, religions can be inherently flawed, as human beings do not always create in Truth. Spiritual truths need to be *lived* and *experienced* to become real and to bring ourselves back to our Spirit within. It is in *being* and *expressing* our inner light, our God within, that we truly live the spiritual principles to which we aspire, whether that comes through a religious approach or not.

If you find religion helpful to your spiritual growth, then by all means continue to go to your place of worship for information, study, and reflection. Nonetheless, keep in mind that it is through searching within and getting to truly know yourself where your spiritual growth really occurs.

Ceremony & Ritual

Ceremony and ritual can play a large part in many spiritual practices. From following a protocol of physical postures like in hatha yoga or performing formal religious rites, to simply lighting incense for meditation, these practices can provide a sense of order and organization from which we can quiet the outside world and turn inward.

When we want to learn to meditate, for example, we may perform a particular ritualistic sequence of tasks such as wearing certain clothing, lighting a candle, bowing before an altar, ringing a bell, lighting incense, playing calming music, repeating affirmations, and counting our breaths. A routine like this can set the tone for our meditation time and help provide a comfortable space where we feel safe. (See *Meditation*) Since meditation is opening the connection to our Higher Self so we can see more clearly with the eyes of Truth, ultimately we want to be able to reach our meditative space without the routine. If we have an attachment to our rituals, then we remain stuck with them as a crutch, limping forward in our growth.

Ceremony and ritual can help set the space for going within and seeing Truth, but they are rooted in the physical world. Although they may help us focus when starting a particular spiritual practice, growing beyond rites and routines means moving toward the feeling and understanding of who and what we truly are beyond anything physical.

Sex

Sex is one of the experiences we can have that comes closest to feeling a union with the divine while in physical form. Two people who are in love who have sex can indeed *make love*, creating a combined energy of union bringing both closer to oneness with all. Physically, it is a pleasurable release that sends a shimmering energy throughout the etheric body, but it is the love genuinely expressed between two people that brings the energy to much higher levels.

When one partner becomes an *object* in the sexual act, there is a blocking of the feeling of true union, which reinforces the energy of separation. Our sense of well-being and groundedness become compromised through this dysfunction in our lower chakras. Furthermore, this objectification of our partner has a lower mental and emotional component (and often an addictive component as well) that distorts the natural sexual union. In most cases, these acts stem from a deep insecurity or inadequacy from early life or past lives that is outpictured into the flesh. What better way to thumb our nose at God than by twisting and debasing a divine act? Ultimately, sex without love reflects how we feel about ourselves.

This is energetically the same for homosexual, bisexual, or other non-heteronormative relationships. In all relations, the more loving, the better.

Finding and nurturing a genuine and loving connection with someone with whom we have sex is something that helps break down the blocks to feeling oneness, helps us be more grounded, and helps support the union with the divine that we seek.

Money

Some people think that being on a spiritual path means living a life of poverty, or at least living with some kind of financial lack. In the past, money and spirituality have often been seen as incompatible. This is not the case, and we perpetuate this myth by thinking so.

Having or earning a great deal of money is not negative. The method of acquiring it, however, can be. If we are less than spiritual in our means of obtaining it, such as through taking advantage of others through deceit, then the conscious or subconscious guilt of doing so tugs our energy downward and creates difficult lessons for us to walk through, if not now, then in future incarnations.

There are many emotions, both conscious and subconscious, that can be associated with having or earn-

Miscellaneous Thoughts

ing a lot of money. Do we feel guilty because our grandparents grew up during the Great Depression and infused our family values with a sense of lack? Did we acquire money dishonestly and feel angry with ourselves for doing so? Are we so attached to it that we are "wealth addicted" and have a fear of losing it? Did we compromise our personal integrity to make money? Are we jealous of our neighbor because he or she makes more than we do? All these things and many more permeate our subconscious beliefs about money, which affect how we earn, view, and spend it.

Commonly, many people regard money with some sense of lack, feeling that they don't have enough and that having more would increase happiness. Studies have shown this to be true up to a point, as a certain level of income can help ease our worries about taking care of basic living needs. However, this still keeps us focused on the three-dimensional level of existence. As spiritual seekers, we desire to take steps to transcend the energies that bind us to the earth plane and move beyond the appearances that leave us in worry, doubt, fear, and scarcity.

Money is a tool that helps us live in this world, just as a car is a tool that helps us travel from one place to another. It is not absolutely necessary, but we would have to adjust how we live without either one of them.

We can experience financial abundance if we let go of any attachment to the idea of it, intend on sufficient resources, *feel* that we have the amount we desire, and then let go of any expectations, trusting that we will be provided for. (See *Intention & Manifesting*) Money and other resources will come, and our needs will be met as we learn to trust ourselves and the energies that work through us for our highest and best. (See *Trust & Discernment*)

Vegetarianism & Other Diets

Someone once asked, "Are you a vegetarian because you love animals or hate plants?"

We certainly want to consume better quality food if at all possible, as well as eat a balanced diet so our physical form has all the nutrients it needs to operate optimally. (See *Care of the Physical*) Buying organic, avoiding fast food, and not oversugaring ourselves are a just few habits that tend to be good for our bodies.

Some believe that eating vegetarian, vegan, or fruitarian makes them more spiritual because the ingested food is lighter and does not have the heavy, trauma-infused energy of slaughtered animals. Indeed, vegetables and fruit *are* lighter in energy, but one must be sure to include appropriate amounts of food that give the body what it needs physically, including proteins, fats, and other nutrients. I have known many vegetarians in and out of my healing practice and most of them have appeared deficient both physically and energetically. One even ate pizza *every* day. Now, there is nothing wrong with pizza (trust me, I'm an expert), but I'm quite sure he had nutritional deficiencies.

If you can get all that your body needs from a particular diet, go for it, but you may want to consult a nutritionist to be sure you are getting the right amounts of critical vitamins and minerals for your body type and activity level. And no, a multivitamin likely does not appropriately fill in the gaps.

For us omnivores, know that the animals that go into the mass-produced meat found on most supermarket shelves are bred for the purpose of consumption. That is their purpose and why they have incarnated. This does not excuse the sometimes terrible conditions in which they live and are slaughtered, which *does* affect the energy of the meat itself. In addition, the multiple rounds of antibiotics and low-grade feed they are often given render the meat bland in both taste and nutrients. Certainly, it is preferable to eat locally-raised, free-range, organic meats.

Trust your gut, literally. I was vegetarian for nearly a year before I was out at a restaurant and decided to break that diet. Actually, I felt like my *body* decided for me, not my mind. I saw the words "prime rib" on the menu and my taste buds instantly exploded, and I was drooling by the time the waiter came by to take my order. As a vegetarian, I often felt like something was missing in my diet, that I could not function quite at my peak. Once I went back to eating meat (that night, and it was delicious!), I began to feel better.

No matter what the diet, the most important thing about eating is to be thankful to the source of the food for its nourishment. It doesn't matter if it is a plant, animal, or insect, being aware of the energy the food provides to sustain our life is to honor and respect nature and the interrelationship of *all* life. Whether you consume meat or not, take a few moments before your meals to appreciate the source of the food. The resonance of your thankfulness will ensure you receive all the energy possible from whatever you consume.

Relationships & Children

Since we have come into these incarnations to learn to love and forgive, there are few experiences that provide the number of lessons and opportunities for growth than intimate relationships. Loving our partner through the ups and downs of life helps us realize the power of love compared to the frivolous details of ego's dramatic distractions.

Intimately sharing our life impels us to look in the mirror at our issues as our mate often reflects that which we are struggling to overcome. Is our anxious or angry partner echoing *our* anxiety or anger? Are they reflecting *our* insecurity with ourselves? An intimate relationship facilitates uprooting these subconscious issues that block our spiritual growth by helping bring them to our awareness.

In addition, relationships rooted in love help foster trust as we become comfortable revealing our true selves to our partner. We find that sharing our belief system and deepest thoughts with them is safe. It may not feel safe at times because we may be challenged, but trusting in the deeper connection, that a surface dispute is just a passing lesson, is paramount for a successful intimate relationship.

Having children will result in even more opportunities for growth. Kids provide the beauty of experiencing every part of the emotional continuum, from intense frustration to inexpressible love. Like with dreams, how we react to the situations that produce those emotions can tell us where we are at our core. (See *Dreams*) Kids also present us with the opportunity for believing in and living for something greater than ourselves. What wouldn't we do for our children, even at great cost or peril to ourselves?

If you tend to avoid close relationships, you will receive lessons through other means. However, great growth occurs through the sustaining love that people in intimate relationships (with partners, kids, or other family) bring to one another. Learning and growing together through love is a magical, transformational experience.

Question:

1. For *each* of the topics presented in this chapter, consider your reaction to what was written. Does it make sense or is the idea challenging? If it *doesn't* fully make sense, explain why you don't think so. If it *does* make sense, how might you apply the information in your life?

~ Chapter 32 ~

Our Choice

We know the truth not only by the reason, but also by the heart.

– Blaise Pascal

Once you make a decision, the universe conspires to make it happen.

– Ralph Waldo Emerson

We can ask for guidance, read more books, attend more seminars, participate in more workshops, or talk about spirituality with our friends, but fundamentally we have a choice to make. That choice is whether or not we are ready and willing to look hard at ourselves, warts and all, and choose to raise our vibration to lighten our energy. It is that simple, but not necessarily easy, and nobody can do it for us. From that choice stems others: to listen to the soft inner voice of our Higher Self instead of the brash voice of the ego; to love instead of fear; to withhold judgments; to detach from outcomes; to forgive others and, most importantly, ourselves; and to fundamentally accept, and thereby remember, who we are as perfect children of God. External information and guidance can help support us in these choices, but we must find the trust to take the leap of faith on our own.

We are blessed to be in human form with guides and angels at our side, so we are never truly alone. With their help, we must choose to minimize and move beyond the ego and its perceived security for the sake of our spiritual awakening. This is no small task, and the rewards may not be tangible initially, but it is the only path back to truly knowing God. It is a path we all are on, even though it might take many, many lifetimes. To know God begins with knowing ourselves, our true selves, who we uncover as we make choices that help us step beyond the influence of the ego.

Even one decision to transcend a situation through love and awareness has rippling effects beyond comprehension. Not only do we lighten ourselves, but others in the situation and others witnessing the situation also experience an energetically positive shift, even if not consciously noticed. It is in these small shifts, as well as in bigger ones, that we become more familiar with our true selves. The effect of these changes, however large or small, ripple throughout humankind as the lighter energy becomes increasingly reflected in our and others' surroundings.

The feeling of choosing to be open and aware can be experienced but not grasped. Grasping only makes it more elusive. It is in being open, without any judgments, fears, or defenses, that we find freedom. To be truly free is to remain open in Truth *continuously*. Then there are no more choices to make, for we have genuinely looked at and accepted ourselves for who we are: a divine being living in the present moment and remembering our way back to God.

The path back to oneness cannot be made without each and every one of us, since everyone and everything in the universe is connected. If we want to change the world, we must start with ourselves, and the world will follow. What are we waiting for?

Questions:

1. Describe how, when, or where in your life you have felt, seen, or experienced this concept.

2. How did you feel as you read the chapter? Did it support or challenge your previous understanding of the material? Explain any changes in how you now view the power of our ability to choose.

3. What stood out to you?

4. What do you feel will help you with your decisions going forward?

5. How might you apply any of this material in your life?

~ Chapter 33 ~

Summary

What springs from earth dissolves to earth again, and heaven-born things fly to their native seat.

– Marcus Aurelius

Below are the bullet point concepts from the Overview that bear repeating. I hope the details on the preceding pages have clarified and given them context.

- No matter how we label it—God, universal intelligence, inner light, Spirit within, etc.—there exists a universal power that is beyond what our conscious mind can comprehend.
- As a seed contains the full potential of the tree, each of us contains all the light, perfection, and potency of God, the universal power.
- We all are on a path of "returning" to our oneness with the divine source, even though we never left it.
- We feel guilt and fear for perceiving that we separated from God, but we never did. God has always been in us and around us in everything that exists, because we are in God.

- The more we remember that God never left us and genuinely live from that perspective, the more we feel and know our divine connection.
- Because God is part of each of us, we as individuals create as God does with God's full and perfect creative power. However, most of the time we *miscreate* because we are not creating out of perfect love in alignment with God.
- The three-dimensional world as we know it is an elaborate illusion, a reflection of mankind's collective conscious and subconscious miscreations and misperceptions. It is a fantasy, like a dramatic television show, because it is not "real life." However, it is the greatest place for us to learn the lessons we need to learn to realize our connection with God.
- What we perceive as our outer world is a mirror of our inner world. Our internal energies invite external circumstances that reflect the sum total of all the energies we carry.
- Both the positive and negative in the three-dimensional world were created by mankind, except for expressions of *perfect* joy, peace, and love, which are divine and beyond illusion.
- The duality of positive and negative becomes subsumed in oneness. There are no opposites in the totality and absolute perfection of the oneness that we know as divine.
- Creating and perceiving from the divinity within us is Truth, which is beyond the physical world. Truth and

illusion cannot coexist because perfect Truth destroys illusion.

- There are no coincidences and no mistakes. Every role has a purpose and every path has merit. Everything we do and experience is for learning to remember our union with God.
- When we can trust in that union and allow the Spirit within to express through us, life becomes joyful and loving as divine guidance unerringly works for our highest and best.
- Time is a three-dimensional concept utilized by mankind to perceive cause and effect. Because only the present moment ever exists, there is no time as we know it. Nevertheless, the progression of time is used as a tool for learning.
- The ego is a non-spiritual aspect of ourselves solely interested in self-preservation. It perceives the increasing awakening to our inner light as a threat to its survival and as such, will subvert our growth at every turn.
- Thoughts, emotions, and memories work together under the direction of the ego to keep us from being truly present in the Now.
- Spiritual growth is about getting closer to recognizing and living from the divine within in the present moment. Always.

The practical suggestions below summarize the preceding chapters. Continuously practicing them will support and enhance our spiritual practice with noticeable results, helping us become more aligned with our Higher Self. By being vigilant to the distractions of our lower mental and emotional bodies and by digging into our subconscious to shine a light on the lower energies of our belief system, we will truly step from merely *existing* in the world to deliberately *living* in it. We will become a beacon of light and an example for others to reflect and emulate.

Choose to consistently put into practice the following:

- Practice grounding, centering, and protecting.
- Meditate daily, even if just for a few minutes.
- Observe your three energies of being and shift to the first.
- Recognize when ego is encouraging you to live from your lower mental and emotional bodies.
- Notice your reactions and reframe situations positively.
- Look honestly at all your beliefs, including those about yourself, others, and the world.
- Let go of perceived karmic bindings and limited belief systems by forgiving everyone and everything, including yourself.
- Know you are a perfect creator in every moment.
- Don't be afraid to ask for help from both physical and non-physical beings.
- Work on making your subconscious conscious with the help of a qualified, professional therapist.

Summary

- Affirm your perfection and divinity in whatever way you are moved to express it.
- Trust your Higher Self over the voice of the ego.
- Love and accept yourself for who you are now, perceived flaws and all.
- Detach from outcomes.
- Reflect on your dreams.
- Get outside and feel your connection to nature.
- Understand that phenomena can be a useful or distracting, unhelpful tool.
- Desire to see and know Truth.
- Choose wisely.
- When you feel you've made a poor choice, simply choose again, without regrets.

See yourself in a mirror and see all the misperceptions that your family, friends, peers, culture, and society have encouraged you to be. See that you are not what *they* think you are. See that you are not what *you* think you are. You are not them. You are not *you* as a personality. You are not your physical body. You are not your thoughts or emotions. You are beyond all that can be conceived of by the concrete mind. *Feel* it, *know* it, and go out into the world confidently seeing the Truth, knowing that this moment is all that exists and that the universe exists within it and within you. For you are divine, seeing with divine eyes, hearing with divine ears, and creating with divine touch. Nothing you encounter is outside of you for you are everything, resonating to all, being all. Remember this and you are truly free.

Questions:

1. What stood out to you?

2. As in Question 3 in Chapter 1, make three columns in your journal (True, Maybe True, and Not True) and classify each bullet point from the beginning of the chapter in the most appropriate column.

3. Does a theme still stand out? Has it changed from the first chapter?

4. Choose five practical suggestions from the twenty given that stand out the most to you.

5. Will you commit to using these suggestions for your spiritual growth? How will you apply each of them? What specific action (or non-action) steps will you take for each?

6. Assess the change in your understanding of spirituality from before reading the book to now. How much is intellectual and how much have you taken into your heart, into who you are?

~ Chapter 34 ~

Not an End, but a Beginning

The moment I have realized God sitting in the temple of every human body, the moment I stand in reverence before every human being and see God in him — that moment I am free from bondage, everything that binds vanishes, and I am free.
— Swami Vivekananda

Man is free at the moment he wishes to be.
— Voltaire

There is a beautiful and clean river not far away that beckons to you. The feeling to go to it is unceasing, and it eventually overwhelms any reasons you have to ignore its call.

You decide to heed its mysterious song and walk toward the scenic waterway. As you approach, you notice that its banks are lined with bushes, thick and barbed, the brambles of distractions in your life. They are the diversions that keep you from doing what you want to do and from being who you want to be. As you make your way to the river, you struggle to avoid them but get caught in the thickets as they reach out, grabbing for you.

As if in a dream, you see that these sharp branches that poke and tear at you have shapes and faces. You see your unsympathetic boss, your cell phone ringing, your unhappy four-year-old self, your partner after your last fight, the toy you couldn't part with as a child, your full email inbox, the overrun garden in your backyard, your annoying commute to work, the maddening details of your upcoming dinner party . . . and yourself, exposed to your fearful core. Your thoughts and emotions reach out and seize your arms and legs as you keep reaching toward the river, leaving you scratched and bleeding. You fight to move forward, progressing slowly and with great pain.

Finally on the riverbank but with the brambles still snatching at you, you step into the water. Immediately, a refreshing feeling begins to wash through you and the branches withdraw. You turn to look at them on the shore and they seem to take on a heavy, almost melancholy quality. You feel sorry for them, for they are so close to the river yet they cannot reach it and feel the serenity of the welcoming water.

Backing slowly into the river, you feel a deep and profound cleansing that extends beyond your physical body. Any emotions dissipate and any remaining thoughts subside. You feel peace to a degree you've never felt before. Still looking at the bushes on the bank, you back up until the water is above your waist. Your hands gently touch the surface and a charge rushes through your veins, electrifying your aura. You pause, feeling the sun and water energizing all levels of your being. Closing your eyes, you trust and know that everything about the river is for your highest good. With that, you fall backwards, allowing yourself to become fully submerged for a moment before coming to the surface to be borne downstream with the current.

As you float, all distractions wash away. You close your eyes and truly *feel*, as if for the first time. There is only you and the river, and you are as one. You float for what seems like eternity.

Eventually, you recognize it is time to return to where you began. You make your way back to the riverbank and see that you will come ashore at the same place you entered. Even though you've been floating down the river for what seems like a long time, you are not surprised. You emerge from the water and begin to slowly walk back to your starting point. Now, the unforgiving brambles are gone, replaced by an easy, walking path winding between soft gardens of flowers and ferns. You pause, enjoying the fresh, light breeze and fragrant landscape.

Looking more closely at the flowers, you now see that they show the same objects and faces as before, but this time there is only love and kindness emanating from them. All previous frustrating qualities are noticeably absent. In fact, the lightness emanating from the objects and faces has such purity that it wipes away any remembrance of the irritations. You can now see them clearly in Truth, as your eyes have been cleansed. You resonate with this light because you carry the illumination from the river within.

Now you notice *yourself* reflected in a particular flower. The beauty and love emanating from the flower, from *you*, is indescribable in its fullness. You never thought you could experience such a feeling of absolute, unconditional love and compassion. You gaze at the flower and finally and truly *know* what lies within.

Viewing the clear path and beautiful field of flowers, you stroll slowly and effortlessly onward to face life as you were meant to, with the light of the river flowing through your body and pulsing in your heart. There is nothing you cannot do. There is nothing you cannot be. All is encompassed in the flowing of the river . . . and it is perfect.

Question:

1. Take a few minutes to silently reflect on all the work you've done in this workbook. What have you learned about yourself?

Not an End, but a Beginning

Congratulations! You've walked through a great deal of material and some questions that may have been deeply personal. If you feel you have uncovered something profoundly challenging, please seek to address it with a counselor or psychotherapist. They can be immensely helpful in guiding you through the process of discerning the lesson, learning from it, and transforming yourself for the better.

Thank you for taking this journey. As it ends, another surely begins.

Thank You

I would like to acknowledge and thank Rev. Penny Donovan, Donald Gilbert, and the Sacred Garden Fellowship community and teachers for helping reframe many years of spiritual study into an understandable whole, my non-physical teachers and guides for never losing faith in me even when I lost faith in myself, and everyone I've interacted with in my life—friends and foes, passing acquaintances and family—whether it was for five minutes or fifty years, for assisting and guiding me in becoming who I am today along the path of learning, loving, and seeing truth, setting the foundation for this book.

About the Author

Peter Santos has been studying spirituality and healing for over three decades while balancing a varied and successful career using his left brain. His extensive travel to sacred sites around the world, including walking the Camino de Santiago in Spain and trekking to sacred Mt. Kailash in Tibet, has grounded the spiritual wisdom he has received, and he is happy to be able to share what he has learned through his writing and teaching. He lives in Vermont.

If you enjoyed this book, please consider leaving a review, as reviews can meaningfully support independent authors like Peter. In addition, you can stay updated on Peter's writings, events, and other projects at www.petersantos.com.

www.ingramcontent.com/pod-product-compliance
Lightning Source LLC
Chambersburg PA
CBHW052018290426
44112CB00014B/2286